WILD RIDE

WILD RIDE

Earthquakes, Sneezes and Other Thrills

BIA LOWE

HarperCollins*Publishers*

Grateful acknowledgment is made to the following publications, in which versions of these essays have appeared:

"Allergy," *Salmagundi,* Fall 1994; "Bats," *The Kenyon Review,* Summer 1992, *Harper's,* January 1993, and *Turning Toward Home: Reflections on the Family from Harper's Magazine,* 1993; "Essential Bodies," *The Kenyon Review,* Summer 1994; "Martian Sighting in Hollywood" was first published as "Martian," *California Quarterly,* Summer 1990; "Mothers and Others, But Also Brothers," *Modern Words,* June 1994, and *Sister and Brother: Lesbians and Gay Men Write About One Another,* HarperSanFrancisco, 1994; "Our Kind," *Western Humanities Review,* Spring 1995; "*Pet,* Noun & Verb" was first published as "Pet," *Lucky,* 1989; "Posterity," *Harbinger,* Beyond Baroque & Silverton Books, 1990, and *Helter Skelter,* Los Angeles Museum of Contemporary Art, 1992; "Wild Ride," *Western Humanities Review,* Autumn 1990, and *Blood Whispers: L.A. Writers on AIDS,* The Gay & Lesbian Services Center and Silverton Books, 1991; "Wings," *Witness* 2, 1994.

Lyrics from the following are reprinted by permission:

"Dancing in the Street" by Marvin Gaye, Ivy Jo Hunter and William Stevenson. © 1964 Renewed 1992 FCG Music, NMG Music, MGIII Music, Jobette Music Co., and Stone Agate Music. All Rights for FCG Music, NMG Music, and MGIII Music controlled and administered by EMI April Music Co. (ASCAP). All Rights Reserved. Used by Permission. "Get Down Tonight" (Harry Casey, Richard Finch) © 1975 Windswept Pacific Entertainment Co. d/b/a Longitude Music Co. International Copyright Secured. All Rights Reserved. Used by Permission. "If My Heart Could Only Talk" (Walter G. Samuels/Leonard Whitcup/Teddy Powell) © Crisscott Music Co., Tee Pee Music Co., Leonard Whitcup, Inc. Used by Permission. "Love Is Here to Stay" (music and lyrics by George and Ira Gershwin) © 1938 (Renewed) Chappell & Co. All Rights Reserved. Used by Permission. "Piece of My Heart" (Bert Berns, Jerry Ragavoy) © 1967 Web IV Music Inc. and Unichappell Music Inc. All Rights Reserved. Used by Permission.

FIRST EDITION

Designed by Nancy Singer

Library of Congress Cataloging-in-Publication Data
Lowe, Bia, 1950–
    Wild Ride : earthquakes, sneezes and other thrills / Bia Lowe.
        p.   cm.
    ISBN 0-06-019053-1
    I. Title.
    AC5.L86   1995
    081—dc20   94-41167

95 96 97 98 99 ❖/RRD 10 9 8 7 6 5 4 3 2 1

For my mother, Barbara

What shall I learn of beans, or beans of me?
—Henry David Thoreau

CONTENTS

Many thanks to Michael Denneny, who first took an interest in my manuscript; to my agent, Malaga Baldi; and to the many talented folks at HarperCollins, particularly Joy Johannessen, Eamon Dolan and Charlotte Abbott.

I am indebted to a community of writers/friends who offered their insights into the making of this book, among them: Leslie Belt, Steve Blakely, Robert Dawidoff, Jacqueline De Angelis, Dana Gorbea-Leon, Terryl Hunter, Rondo Mieczkowski, Linda Norlen, Aleida Rodríguez, Jane Thurmond, David Vernon and Terry Wolverton; and especially Susan Anderson, Bernard Cooper and Michelle Huneven, who are most arduously in my corner.

ALLERGY

Like orgasm, 90 percent of a sneeze is sheer anticipation. You're balanced fifty feet up, the rope under your feet is wobbling like crazy and it's only a matter of time before you fall. This peril would be both exhilarating and unbearable, like the perfect arc in sex you want to sustain forever, if only you weren't so greedy. Then the fall comes. In sex, it's hair-splitting contractions and the blood spilling back into the rest of your body. In a sneeze, your body is an archer's bow letting fly an exhalation of up to a hundred miles per hour. A sneeze can be the body's most succinct release, provided, of course, it performs its function—to blast the respiratory irritant to kingdom come.

But suppose no amount of honks, even at hurricane force, could do it; no limit to the globs of mucous shot like bullets, no end to gesundheits. Suppose the body was required to fire an exhaustive battery of sneezes, like an unrelenting succession of orgasms, leaving you no more resolved, but rather, breathless, swollen, gun-shy.

Normally, we breathe an average of twelve times a minute, and the swelling of our ribs seems as inevitable as the breaking of day. Of course this wasn't always so; at one time our chests were as sealed as jelly jars. Our mothers once did all the breathing for us. Only after we slithered through the watery membrane were we able to gasp and snortle, like our scaly forebears, into this world of air.

Once we're here we scarcely give our respiration a second thought, unless we're watching a skin diver or an astronaut—air tanks strapped securely to their backs—as they tumble bravely through lethal depths. Breath or *pneuma* was once believed to be the primal element of the universe, milk of the cosmos. No wonder that when we sneeze even a stranger will offer up a "God bless you," as though that superstitious tic could save us from asphyxiation, and fill our lungs once more, like sails.

■ ■ ■

Now the hay mill is a rusted relic, but back in the days of my childhood it chewed up bales of alfalfa and spit the little bits up through a stovepipe and into a door in the loft of the barn. The tiny blown blades settled into a two-story pile on the barn floor. Sometimes hollows, enormous bubbles, formed within that pale green mountain. The round walls of those pockets made for cozy forts, if they were large, or kitten dens, if they were small. Green dust blanketed everything. Every surface in the barn, even the hairline edges of chicken wire, supported a ledge of green.

After hours of playing in the barn, the insides of my ears, eyes and nose were caked with powder, and the back of my throat tasted of alfalfa. At dusk I returned home to shower before dinner and, standing before the length of our bathroom mirror, saw how my naked body had been ornamented in what seemed like olive Crayola. A thick line of green ran from navel to sternum, drew ovals around my armpits, shaded the under-side of my shoulderblades, and traced the indention of my spine until it caked into the Y of my buttocks. Eventually I would become allergic to the barn, weeping as I swung out from the loft on a rope, sneezing as I tumbled on the mountain made of alfalfa, wheezing as I dug my forts.

Adolescence distilled my grass allergies into a literal spring fever as, brimming with both hormones and histamines, I wept knee deep in fields of mustard. My trusted meadows somehow transformed into mine fields. All the secret hiding places in the barn were off-limits. Play, the rough and tumble, the sorcery of tomboys, ended as definitively as the barn door sliding shut.

■ ■ ■

What's it like to have asthma? You'd know if you ever fell from a jungle gym, the air slammed out of you, your ribs straining to reopen the collapse. You'd remember how you had fallen out of time, the seesaw of your breathing shushed, your body trying to suck the rhythm back. It's as if my lungs are paper sacks, the stuff I cough up a dead ringer for Jell-O, and nothing, not even my mother, is as important as my next breath.

■ ■ ■

Histamine is released when a cell is injured. Histamine affects circulation, dilating capillaries and arterioles, bringing a sudden flow of blood to the injured cell. In the case of allergy, something deep within the body, within the cells, claims the injury, and sets off a kind of alarm. The sufferer of an allergy is often at a loss to understand why her body would identify the most unassuming of influences, say a puppy, as a threat. Here I am, a lifelong nature zealot, but my body, turned suddenly paranoid, declares war on my religion daily. My allergy confines me like barbed wire to the realms of the shorn, the scrubbed, the paved. It seems I need protection, but from *whom?*

By my twenties my immune system found a new culprit in the animal kingdom. Now dogs, cows, horses—even my beloved feline roommate—make me wheeze and tear. I persist however, out of devotion, but suffer the consequences. And as the years of sneezes accrue, as my breathing grows more labored, I've felt an involuntary estrangement. Now when I see an animal, I know I'm a tourist in hostile terrain. No matter how luscious the fur, how soulful the eyes, there's danger lurking for me. Gone are the days at the slope of a horse's neck, the velvet of his muzzle, those lips working my palm like a chamois glove. Gone the steaming mornings, my forehead at the belly of the cud chewer, my fingers pulling her teats like a rapacious lover. Gone are the canine days, the days of tongues, and his smell like roasted peanuts. Gone the sultry lashes of burros, the glistening nostrils of calves. Who is it who removed me to this remote island, who marooned me to a vast sea of mucous, a sky full of irritability? Why has my body uprooted me from my home?

■ ■ ■

On the ranch, cruelties were as commonplace as passing the butter. Lambs' tails were clipped like branches. Birds were blasted out of the air. Fish were clubbed, kittens drowned. It was no time to get soft. Better, much better, to stave off the shock for later.

Allergens are derived from some form of life. Proteins from, say, a calf's saliva, act to stimulate the allergic state, which throws the body into a kind of shock. The shock tissues in humans are the mucous membranes, the bronchial tubes, the intestines or the skin. These areas swell and are accompanied by surrounding redness and itch.

Occasionally one of the foreman's sheepdogs wouldn't perform. Maybe too stubborn, maybe not smart enough. Then I'd see him being dragged by a leash into the back field, each step resisting the pull at his neck, tail tight against his buttocks, head cowering at the heels of the man holding a rifle.

Fluid appears, covering the outer elastic membrane of the cornea, protecting it against microorganisms, pollution or dust. Seawater, ancestral solvent, is secreted by the lachrymal glands, and spills from the eye. The mucous membranes swell to block the entry of offending particles or gases. Orifices drain, flushing away invasive proteins. Noses run, blisters brim, eyes tear.

I often pedaled down the dirt road that ran the length of the pasture while Little Bull's hooves tore up the grass on the other side of the fence. For the two years we raced each other, I never let myself think what would inevitably happen to the foreman's calf. Then one day I skidded to a stop in front of the dog-houses. Little Bull's head was lying in the dust within the radius of the dogs' chains, his eyes dull with grit. The rest of him, I discovered later, had been butchered, wrapped and stored in a large freezer. Each organ was labeled by hand. I lifted one package: LITTLE BULL'S LIVER, another: LITTLE BULL'S HEART.

An inner wind, a quiet wail pushes inside the throat. An inability to articulate thoughts mounts like a nimbus. All stimuli, even light, join the ranks of irritants. A kind of lassitude takes hold. There is blushing, heat, redness in the face. A noise seizes the inside of the chest, a rasp caused by convulsive catching of breath. (Is this sobbing about the kittens? the dogs? the calf? If I could have my fill of crying would I be cured?)

■ ■ ■

Let me set the scene and go back in time to the days when all eyes were tracking Halley's comet and feet were moving to the syncopation of ragtime. Suddenly we find ourselves face-to-face with something called the unconscious. A physician in Vienna has patients who are powerless in its grip. These Victorians are stricken with hysterical paralysis, false pregnancies, symptoms accrued against a lifetime of denial. The bearded doctor approaches the couch, carrying Pandora's box like a Whitman's sampler, and asks each patient to lift the lid and taste.

Since then our legacy has been one of mistrust—when we hear a wheeze we wonder . . . icebox mother? passive father? family unit in the throes of dysfunction? Which ancient Gorgon can be held responsible for our fucked-up lives? If asthma is a way of crying "wolf," histrionics performed for the benefit of one's parents, can't a heart-to-heart with Mom, or even a meditation in the form of an essay get to the bottom of it?

Before we lose ourselves in a convolution of self-analysis, let's not forget that these were also the coal-burning days, the steam-hissing days, the days of the "civilized world" and the electric light bulb. We sped behind the wheel of a Tin Lizzie, humming songs like "Come Josephine, in My Flying Machine," all the while choking on the air. A guy like Chaplin could have been mangled in the gears of a factory, or killed just as easily by newly discovered dangers he couldn't see, like germs, viruses, radiation. Our age requires a mistrust of the senses, of institutions, of slogans, and especially of ourselves.

Did allergies become epidemic with the Industrial Revolution? With the sullying of our skies, the overtaxing of our immune systems? Are they flourishing because our concept of nature has become too abstract, viscera packaged tidily in Saran, continents smoothed into a pastel patchwork? Or because we are our own saboteurs, unwitting pawns of treacherous emotion?

■ ■ ■

Who knows what triggers alarm in my cells, what scours my bronchioles until the chambers fill like blisters. Life being what it is in Los Angeles, it might be emotional stress, the stage-two smog alert, foods so packed with additives they read like a recipe for a new life-form. I envy those who thrive on Twinkies and car exhaust, marching heartily into tomorrow, their eyes a deeper shade of Blue Number 2. Should I think of myself as a wimp too sensitive for the future, too inflexible for mutation, obsolete as a dinosaur? Or as a canary in the coal mine, my gasps and wheezes cautionary signals for hardier folk.

My allergies worsen in summer when the L.A. air is rank, the downtown banks barely peeking over striations of orange, khaki, and violet. I feel a dull pain as my lungs expand to their breadth, as though the outer lining had been worn, like brake pads, down to metal. I adapt to shallow breathing. And when I try to clear the phlegm from my throat, I sound like I'm trying, without success, to turn my engine over.

■ ■ ■

These days the body is something to be mastered, driven like a Maserati. And the mind, rather than busying itself with transcendence, sits imperiously in the driver's seat, foot to the floor, dreaming of a full tank of gas. Our waking nightmare is a body not customized to fit our preferred self-image. Breasts are too large, penis too small, lips not full enough, skin never the right hue. The surgeon who once might have extricated deadly tumors is now in the business of sculpting special effects. Hair relocates from neck to crown, genitals are reconfigured and rehung, and fat is siphoned off to the junk heap. We are at war with our flesh, at war with machines that inevitably rattle and rust, with matter that always surrenders to entropy.

Of course, wouldn't it be wiser simply to excuse the hulking oaf? Excuse the one who can not fit into a size seven, whose genitals are all wrong, whose farts overwhelm crowded elevators, who sweats too readily and sneezes too frequently? Excuse the one who becomes ill or simply grows old? Wouldn't it be better to find oneself in the embrace of a great spiritual body, instead of the sag of our impossible physiques?

Our bodies are out of our control, helmed by mutinous sailors. How else can we possibly be growing old? What ship will rescue us when this one runs aground?

■ ■ ■

Someday I may move away to a less threatening environment. There'll be clouds in the sky and breeze enough for clothes to swell on a clothesline. Someday when I'm aged and the ravages of hormones have taken their toll, the histamines too may settle, quiet down like a war-weary army, and I'll return to my childhood companions. Perhaps then, as a grand old dame, I'll have Angora rabbits perched on every surface, their hair choking every fabric, the smell of pee drenching the air. My knit pants will be swaddled in dog fur, tufts hanging from my sweater like clumps of mown grass. Every hooved creature will snow dander onto my carpets. Flurries will rise and settle as I walk through rooms, and trees will send me their sexy missives, as spores and pollens waft through the open windows. Open windows, that's what I crave. The sight of a ship on the horizon, its sails gorged with air.

WILD RIDE

We were both dropouts, both had floundered in our first year of college and ended up affluent and directionless back in the Bay Area the year after the Summer of Love. He would stop by my pad around two, after seeing his therapist. With his long greasy hair, long wrinkled rain-coat, hollow eyes and high-tops, he was every bit the image of Ichabod Crane meets William Burroughs. I was, in my overalls, work shirt, long hair and fringe jacket, the very image of Emma Goldman meets Annie Oakley. We'd walk around the city and smoke joints, talking about the corruption in all things Amerikan. The subtext in our conversations was a rebellion against sex roles—a sentiment that was finding its legs with flower power and would soon find its voice with the sexual movements of the seventies. We were struggling to be *not* well adjusted, to discover the selves beneath our years of cotillions, prep schools and proper manners. We elevated childhood as the purer form, a realm where the noble savage romped, uncoerced by the "adult" enterprises of Hugh Hefner or the strip joints in North Beach. We were resisting assimi-lation, holding fast to our polymorphous perversity, reclaiming arrested development.

He collected children's books, I collected toys. We were brother and sister in a family for which we had no name.

But this is not another homosexual story. I was intend-ing to write about Clark because I'm trying to fathom his death. The way one grapples with the meaning of a dream, by lowering a net and bringing its life writhing to the surface.

Dreams often concern death, or the threat of it. The colossal fist of the ocean looms above me, or I'm unable to stop my speeding car though my foot presses, presses the brake. Shrinks would tell me, and have, that these are symbolic representations of feeling states. They don't necessarily mean I'm afraid of the ocean or that I'll die in a car accident. But sometimes I wonder: out of the many dreams I have, couldn't *one* be prescient? Isn't it possible for some dreams to depict not mere representations but literal truths? And if so, which dream should I pay attention to? Will there be a time when I'm unable to stop my car and the useless flooring of the brake will seem nightmarishly familiar?

■　■　■

There is a ride at Disneyland, a mad ride in an old jalopy, where every wrench in the road is a kind of ticklish jeopardy. And as you career past each hazard, each more hair-raising than the last, you wonder where will it end? When will the hilarity turn to deadpan adrenaline? Cops pop up from nowhere blowing whistles. Brick walls wobble precariously, and as you rush seemingly headlong into them, they unhinge. You even blast into a courtroom barely missing the judge who swears by heaven he'll sentence you for speeding. But finally you swing screeching into a tunnel, and you realize, perhaps because it's so dark, that this part of the ride is different. Up ahead, the approaching sound of a locomotive and the headlight of its engine bring on the ice of alarm. Surely your car will swerve before you collide? You never suspect that your car will keep going, that the collision will be quiet, painless, that you will keep speeding through the dark.

I try to imagine what it means to be dead. As a child I used to believe that when you died your mind lived on as though nothing had happened. That if, say, you died in a car accident, your immortal mind would imagine you unharmed in the wreckage, that you would continue your business, finish the grocery shopping, return to the ones who love you. Sometimes still I wonder if this might not be true. How could the ego with all its dazzle and demands simply go poof in the night? A whole luminous life like a dove into a top hat?

And sometimes, especially when I'm driving, I wonder if I might already be dead, if my body has already been struck down, and my experience is really propelled by imagination alone. Undying imagination, like a movie in a dark theater.

■ ■ ■

I watched my cat Lucy die, my companion of fifteen years. Lucy and I kissed each other on the lips and then the vet gave her the drugs. She was out but not yet dead, he said, she had a few minutes left. So I whispered things in her ear, the kinds of things people talk about these days—move towards the light, let this life go, become one with the universe. Her eyes were so dilated they seemed, like the universe, to contain a kind of impending indifference, a hard-edged void that tunneled its way, like the ride at Disneyland, into a continual dark. Then I noticed the cornea of her eyes change from something wet and glassy to something dryer, stippled, already transforming. She was gone. Her body sagged like a puppet with no hand inside it. Whatever held her many cells together was devolving.

All the night before I kept her company, watched her struggle with her pain. And though I wouldn't allow her to, she wanted to go outside, to die as cats know how, alone.

Being human, I couldn't bear it. Dying alone is unthinkable—to be like a beetle on one's back, all arms raking the air, desperate for familiar ground. Or perhaps it's unthinkable because dying *is* being alone, mourning the companionship of one's delusory glory. The full blaze of a life cools and condenses into simple carbons, the beetle succumbs finally to the inglorious appetites of soil. And there's a distinct lack of applause.

I have a photograph of my father and me the year before he died, the year before the Summer of Love. I'm sixteen and he's fifty-three, though he looks at least seventy. He is drinking himself to death. Of course I have the advantage of hindsight, and everything about his appearance is a warning flare to me now, a quarter of a century later. I see he is trying to step out of the picture, away from me and his wife, who is clicking the shutter. He is moving, like the cat, toward a picture in which there is nothing but isolation. I also am trying to escape the picture because his isolation dominates it, and because a part of me has already felt his death, like dreams I laugh off though I keep glancing over my shoulder. I am moving away from him because I am young, and I won't look at what I know.

But back to Clark. The fact of the matter is, Clark and I grew apart. After those few years in San Francisco I moved away to go to school in another city, and ultimately to find my tribe among lesbians. He grew muscles and followed the Dionysian path. Where the sixties had joined us as siblings, the seventies segregated us into distinct species, ghettoized by our sexualities.

Occasionally we'd get together, but I found him petty. An hysteric. I think he probably felt my politics had made me twisted and humorless. If you had asked me in the seventies how Clark would die, I probably would have sneered "too much sex." Then, I would have thought that a lifestyle like a ride in a wild jalopy could come to no good. But now I question that kind of judgment. Now I question a world spun by moral causality. Now I wonder if, say, the rails on that ride were cracked, if Chaos stood behind the curtain slamming levers, cranking gears, would it matter how slowly, how safely you tried to drive? If, say, something was senseless and awry with the mechanism, if the brick wall refused to unhinge and AIDS was something you got in the pursuit of love, what good is a brake?

The point, if there is one, is this: life makes us scream with apprehension and delight; if it doesn't, perhaps the ride we're on isn't wild enough. And while part of the body prepares for death, while part of the body is wise to the figure behind the curtain, pulling fractals, cranking the unforeseen, our throats are hoarse with wild laughter and our eyes stream in the thrill of it.

Clark's life toward the end was very full. I'd get evidence of its richness in the mail, stories he'd written for the "People With AIDS" newsletter, a Christmas card he'd made. I'm looking at that card right now, an exuberant display of arrested development. On the front, a color photograph of Clark and his infant niece dressed up like dinosaurs, surrounded by dinosaur stuffed animals. Inside it reads, "Joyous Eleanorasaurus and Klarkus Crayolatops love you."

He worked at having a family, at rebuilding the very thing that had sent him into therapy two decades earlier. And here he is, a dying man with a baby, dressed like an extinct creature, having the time of his life.

I was told he had his family with him. They listened to his labored breathing, whispered into his ear about letting go, stared into a dark eye already turned inward in search of light. They watched as his story fizzled into the ether like the snowdrifts of television.

A few months later I received a packet of wildflower seeds in the mail, a posthumous gift Clark had arranged for his friends.

I mixed the seeds with sand to help them scatter in my garden. It's the same dirt I buried Lucy in. The same dirt that holds the bones of two other cats before her. The dirt of decomposed things—rock, bark, beetles, cats, dinosaurs.

There's one last thing about the ride at Disneyland. It doesn't end with the dark tunnel. There's more. A blast of hot air, and the dark cracks open into a riotous bacchanal of demons, hot-pink devils with midriff bulges who bob on walls of lava. They are having, as it were, the time of their lives. A great time, devilishly good. A happy ending to a ride that had been altogether too abbreviated.

I'd like to think that life is resolved in such a place. Not the ethereal retirement home to which all earthly pleasures have been sacrificed, nor the pit of damnation in which the fundamentalists envision the likes of Clark forever wheeling on a rotisserie. I like to think of a place more lively, a place that has no respect for the dead, oblivious to reward or punishment, a place that has no regard for you or me or the Bible—a place in the earth, a bacchanal of jocular mildews, horny pollens, ribald bacteria, an arena suitable for the most high-minded of noble savages, full of elemental stuff, seeds, bones, mold.

For the last few winters Disneyland has been hosting a fundraiser for the AIDS Project in L.A. Once a year thousands of homosexuals drive to Anaheim for "Gay Night." If there ever was a more raucous show of arrested development, I've never heard of it. Shrieks and gales of laughter echo through the fog of the Magic Kingdom.

After leaving Mr. Toad's Wild Ride, my friend Brian and I head for the Haunted Mansion. There is a long line in front of us that snakes its way through the cemetery. And as we stand in the stream of leather jackets and giggle at the names on the tombstones, "D. Ceest," "Diane Gontahevon," etc., Brian tells me this joke:

A little boy runs to his mother and asks, "Mommy, is it true that when we are born we come from dust?"

The mother says, yes.

"And Mommy, is it true that when we die we go back to dust?"

The mother says, yes, that's right. From dust to dust.

"Well, Mommy, come upstairs and look under my bed 'cause someone's either coming or going."

POSTERITY

I'm in my forties, tempted to visualize myself at the middle distance, poised at the topmost step of a staircase, the climbed years behind me, the descending years ahead. And what I see from the landing at the top of this stairway is a world nearly packed with people my own age, each grasping a banister, each suspended awkwardly in midlife, unable to account for the time that has vaulted us there. It's as if we've risen above the haze of the city, above the dome of clouds, into a calm beyond the timberline, where we can see finally a view that dwarfs our singular roosts. And from this perch we wonder, as the Himalayan monks must, what's the meaning of it all? We sway as we contemplate our decline, as we follow the darkening rail down the stairs into the basement.

Childhood was our common mythology, an upbeat realm where immortal cherubs devised their pranks and basked in the forgiveness of Olympian parents. Weaned on a cathode ray, bawling for Bosco, we drummed our rattles into the sparkling carpet, gleeful to see our own reflections in the face of Beave. Who would have dreamed Mom would die in the midst of a settlement with the studios? Or Pop would drop from a pickled liver? Big Sis is as old as Mom ever was, and coked Bro's a chauffeur to the stars.

Age is scrambling the signal. Twisting the dials won't fix it, an epidemic of ghosts confounds the picture. We're spooked by ghosts and the riddles even monks can't unravel; so we step through the mirror, mount a winding staircase of DNA onto a landing littered with Huggies and rainbow ponies. Here's a view to remember: one's own spitting image, hope for a future.

Once upon a time my development reflected the majority around me; but now there's a brood of offspring, a chorus of hasty answers to an impossible riddle.

■ ■ ■

I remember when I last held the family album, a grand tome bound in caramel leather. I was taking Lilly on a pictorial tour of my past. Lilly! Age seventeen, the first throb to burst the cherry in my Sapphic heart. Like all teenagers, we were fascinated with our childhoods—fueled with the indignation of dime-store psychology, but also saddened to be entering into a world of cold choice and corruption, closing the door on our child-lives forever.

We examined the photographs with the same bittersweet eyes Holden Caulfield had for his sister, Phoebe, and I was sure then that I would reproduce a child like the one caught inside the wavy borders of those Polaroids. I alone could mother that child—after all, her needs matched exactly my need to have them fulfilled.

There would be then a childhood spiraling without conclusion, the small hands curling themselves like question marks around my fingers, my eyes answering hers with a similar green. Lilly is now in her forties and has two sons and never has time to finish a complete sentence on the phone.

I stand alone on an imagined staircase, nursing sentences as if the best of me could at last feel its own flesh.

■ ■ ■

Now if I had a child, a true human child, not a cat or a garden or a body of poems, I would do more than love her. I would take her on walks as my own mother did. We would walk through the city, past lawns where each day mushrooms rise uninvited, past dogs that roam with their nostrils at the pavement. We would walk into the countryside until we found a river. We would sit there and talk and eventually we would talk about sex. But unlike my own mother, I would approach the subject by trying to explain orgasms.

I would tell her that orgasm in the man is a time when he launches thousands of sperm into the world, where all but one swim to their deaths in the dream of finding the golden egg and being reborn. When women orgasm they are like a stream that pools, so that the fish that leap and climb on stairs of air can rest, and spawn finally at their source.

In this way I hope I will have described a difference between male and female: how his moment carries the imperative of the species' survival; how her egg moves through her as a matter of course, independent of sex or its conclusion. How her journey is singular, ongoing, like the egg, but also encompassing like the river; how his journey is heroic and competitive like the fish. I would remind her that she is made of both ova and sperm, that the memories of her beginnings will move her in these ways, both female and male.

But finally I would mention that orgasms, like sex, involve pleasure, and that she will have this pleasure again and again without having to travel backward in time to that slow place in the river where a cell grew lungs amid soft threads of algae. And that pleasure, like language, exists in a different season than all the biological stairs, helixes, ladders and landings.

And I would suspect that she herself had probably discovered this, bravely with a friend perhaps, or alone in the dark. And I would propose to her that there must be a reason for pleasure of this sort, a reason for desire itself, which so seldom has anything to do with procreation, but which has labored more sentences than offspring, and which seeks to resolve itself again and again like a riddle between the movement of two bodies, or even in solitude.

I'm sure all this would puzzle her as I hope it would, and months later, we would walk back to that river, through the city, past houses where families are stringing their Christmas lights and the rain-wet sidewalks smell of pepper, and we would stare at the river which would be roiling with gravel and mud.

OUR KIND

for Lucy

A forest contains my earliest memories. A dark woods, where trees kept the sky at bay, the sort through which Gretel or Goldilocks might wander. Underneath the fir dome my small voice echoed, then faded. I liked the bark of redwoods, it was shaggy, the color of dried blood. Humus crushed like Shredded Wheat beneath my feet, and sent up the stinging scent of Christmas, even in August.

Stumps the size of elephants hulked in the shadows, evidence that this forest, like much of coastal Mendocino, was once the land of titans before it was logged. Our cabin and its environs were simple. There was a wooden platform a few yards away where my older brothers pitched their tent each year. And another structure, farther off, a mysterious shack called the "powerhouse," where my father went evenings to generate electricity for the cabin and the canopy of Japanese lanterns on our deck. He emerged from these rites, red-faced and sweaty, the solemn generator droning like a Gregorian chant.

Our redwood deck tucked itself like a collar under the face of the cabin, and stuck out thirty feet above the Noyo river. The rest, the woods stretching in all directions from us, was wilderness. As far as I could see, interrupted only by the serpentine cleft of the Noyo, were vaulting redwoods. And beyond them, darkness.

Twice each day a train called the Skunk huffed its way past us, metered the day into chunks of time. It was a child's paradise, laying pennies on the tracks, tagging behind my brother Peter as he brought groceries back from the train platform in a wheelbarrow. I spent hours naked among the river rocks, waving to the Skunk as it heaved across the trestle, while my brothers tried in vain to snipe water striders with their Daisy BB guns.

Then each fall the windows were sealed, the doors shut. We wheeled our belongings to the train platform, and waited for the Skunk to carry us seaward, eleven miles back to Fort Bragg. The long seasons spent in that lumber town are lost to me. While my brothers resumed their school lives, I might as well have been curled in hibernation.

At the end of spring we'd return to find the river rerouted, our paths eclipsed by brush and debris. The Noyo often left a calling card of mud on the floor of the cabin, the boys' platform camouflaged in a snarl of tree limbs webbed with rags. Sometimes farther downriver a derelict car lay upturned like a bug, torpedoed by river rock. The sheer brawn and ferocity of the wilderness was thrilling, but made me feel small and kept me within earshot of the cabin.

I was told the shadows of these woods were rife with bears— not the shackled variety in circus acts, nor the clownish totems fashioned for children with fur, felt and kapok—but *real* bears. Bears who lap grubs from rotted wood, who grin and smack as they relish a chipmunk, a woodchuck, a comb of honey, a cricket. Bears who "yarr," humping one another on the soft forest floor, who rake the shallows of the Noyo for steelhead, who rummage through trash for candy bars. Bears whose scats are studded with seeds and aluminum foil.

■ ■ ■

They are called same-size predators, omnivores who, like us, binge on the receiving end of the food chain. So there exists a kind of horizontal hostility between us, a mutual respect, a regard straddling both rivalry and identification. Voracious gourmands, bears would be at home foraging through the kitchens of prestigious restaurants, bolting pork chops glazed with port, salads of bitter greens and wild mushrooms, whole warm tartlettes of pear and Gorgonzola, their eyes gleaming while berries and drips of chocolate hang from their lips.

And when they stand and display their bulk, either to intimidate or to flirt, they look like us, like beer-bellied uncles in long johns or zaftig aunties eager to dissolve us in their cumulus bosoms. Who can resist that emblem of coziness when the female is snuggled with her snoozing cubs, the den sawing with snores? Or when, ambling out onto April grass, the cubs bask in mama bear's constant supervision. The cubs are ourselves at our most vulnerable, flouncing through a protracted childhood, dependent on the intimacies of the maternal bond.

Hairless, blind and 1/625th of its adult weight, a bear cub is born virtually defenseless. Through play with its mother it learns the facial expressions and body postures that make up its social lexicon, the occasional social graces so necessary to a shy and solitary adult. Accompanying its mother, the cub learns the secrets of how, when, and where to fish, to gather, to hunt, and even to bed. These are imitators, trusting souls, whose very submission to sleep is wholehearted, and requires guidance.

And as we are the greatest imitators of all, child after human child falls into bed clutching a worn toy cub. It's a ceremony in which we reenact the bear's maternal bond, and make our descent into the den. The bear is a fellow traveler, a chum on the journey to the underworld.

In those days on the Noyo, I had a teddy bear. What was left of his cinnamon fur was whorled, and his eyes, into which I could gaze for hours, were emerald star bursts. Each morning I woke with Teddy, each day he accompanied me. I was a small and solitary creature in the woods, too young to be on equal footing with my brothers. While my family conversed on a stratum beyond my comprehension, Teddy was the audience for my soliloquies. His threadbare pelt gave into the pressure of my embraces, and smelled of my skin. By nightfall, as the forest groaned above my ceiling, Teddy's unblinking profile was beautiful across my pillow. I slept safely with that fetish tucked into my bed, while muscular gods teemed in the dark beyond our deck.

Until my brother killed him. Why my brother murdered my bear is anyone's guess. Perhaps his bear met the same fate years before. Perhaps to certify his graduation from immature attachments. Perhaps, simply, to test his capacity for cruelty. "Teddy looks sick," Richard proclaimed. "He needs an operation." What did I know; Richard was older, therefore wiser. After what seemed like hours, Richard emerged from his tent and announced the surgery had been unsuccessful. Teddy did not pull through. His pale innards lay in lumps around his deflated body and showed me the insubstantial nature of magic. Idols could be toppled, spells broken, wishes could come to nothing. Part of my child's ego had been excised in that operation. After witnessing the heaps of cotton, where was I to find security?

My mother rushed to the scene like a paramedic, and carried off Teddy's corpse to the cabin. A few hours later my bear was restored to me. A flannel heart had been sewn over the awful gash, and on that heart my mother had stitched "I Love You." And though those words were emblazoned on *his* heart, *her* love resounded through them like the voice of a ventriloquist.

Teddy had risen from the dead to represent love to me, but he could never again embody it. It was too late. His death estranged us, made me aware, once and forever, that the pretense of our interaction was childish. I would never be able to believe in him so wholeheartedly. The world was a place where talismans can turn to sham. Something inside me had callused. I would spend the rest of my days untangling romance from unreality. And I would understand that I too could inflict the sting of cruelty. I had been punctured, torn a bit; but like a cub, I was learning the ferocious lessons of my kind.

■ ■ ■

Some cabins in Alaska have huge spikes on their shutters facing outward, prohibiting bears from simply smashing their way in. Occasionally one hears stories of campers shredded by grizzlies, of trailers ripped open exposing the inhabitants like canned goods. There are legends of men who've done battle with bears, mostly nineteenth-century macho showmen like John Capen (Grizzlie) Adams, who after a career of wrestling bears said, "I have been beaten to a jelly, torn almost limb from limb, and nearly chawed up and spit out by these treacherous grizzly bears." In the end, it was a grizzly who laid him out cold, a pet grizzly who evened the score.

Of course no bear can match the sheer meanness of a gun, or the cold-hearted barbarity of a steel trap. There are no predators more bloodthirsty, indeed more inhumane, than we. But even saying so softens its edges. We've confessed our cruelties a thousand times, like a thousand Hail Marys, until remorse softens into balm.

Even our *idea* of bears atrophies as surely as their numbers dwindle. Who is the bear? Affable uncle, or homicidal monster? Patient mother or howling nightmare? The bear is, of course, neither—and a bit of both. The bear eludes us, her intelligence as incomprehensible as the blank before the Big Bang, but her passions—the lair's defense, the groin's spasm, the unguent delectability of honey—are as wholly felt as our own.

Imagine your brain whirring quietly like a hard disk, without the body, its attendant fleshy companion. No one to confound it with pleasure, love or mortality. No one, in effect, to person-alize it. This, I think, is the world without beasts. Large beasts, dangerous and elegant.

In tribal times, the creatures with whom we shared the forest were gods. Through the rituals of hunting we heard their songs and sang back to them. We were open, trusting, and religious. Those we revered were reflections of our own needs, our hungers, our fears. The whole *megilla*, animal-vegetal-mineral (even the temporal) was coddled in the amniotic goo of subjec-tivity. The contours of our bodies blurred with the landscape. We knew the animals as we knew our own dreams.

Now we're floating like astronauts, tumbling through a dark voided of purpose. The tidy surfaces of our technology have marooned us in spectacular cities, manufacturing fantasies that increasingly exclude the existence of animals. The totems we give our children are mutating into something altogether un-crea-turely. Yogi Bear begat Daffy Duck begat Kermit begat Barney. What next? What forms, if any, will the wildness in us take?

■ ■ ■

My parents eventually sold the cabin in the redwoods and bought a summer home farther south, an old sheep ranch about ninety minutes from what San Franciscans modestly call The City. The Alexander Valley, now famous for its vineyards, was then a hodgepodge of hop yards, prune orchards, and pas-tureland. Sloping above these cultivated flats were the oak-splashed hills, golden in summer, green in the rainy season, var-iegated with wildflowers in spring.

We had a garden, which replaced the powerhouse in my father's production of sweat. He took two years to build a rock wall around the garden, with rocks the boys hauled up from the creek. His body was perpetually cantilevered over that wall, an upside-down L, and a gleaming drop of perspiration miraculously clung to the tip of his nose. We planted trees, hedges, and rototilled an area for vegetables.

In a broader sense of the word, much of the ranch was a garden. Old groves of fir and redwood had been shorn into pastures. Barbed wire broke the hills into sections. An irrigation lake had been dug, roads scraped and graveled, and domestic animals, mostly sheep, waddled and coughed and grew fat. It was a far cry from the dense woods of Mendocino county.

Though the wide-open landscape let the sun in and seemed benign, I was warned of creatures that might be lurking in the brush: snakes, wild pigs and bobcats.

My old devotion to Teddy had been eclipsed by the rough and tumble of fantasy games and by the companionship of farm animals. There was Shorty the geriatric nag, and Little Bull, the pup trapped inside the body of a steer. Yet wild creatures always held the strongest fascination for me, the very ones I had been cautioned against, ones who left paths along slopes. Whose lurid turds sometimes gleamed with seeds. Whose hairs could be found on the trunks of trees, caught in a rasp of bark.

I was looking for messages, dispatches not only from them, but from someone deep within my own body. As my Keds carried me soundlessly through gullies, my wiles outsmarting those creatures who had always eluded me, I was savoring the sharp flavors of predation. I tasted stealth, visual acuity, heightened sense of smell and hearing. My body became specialized for the prowl, eloquent in tactical movement, and focused power. I was as self-assured as a cougar or a bear. Now sometimes, when a wind kicks up, the same thrill takes hold of me, makes me want to spring like a cat, or disappear into the brush of my garden.

■ ■ ■

I live in Los Angeles, a semiarid desert, as distinct a landscape as you can get from the verticality of an ancient conifer forest. It is precisely this horizontality, the sensation of latitudes without limit, that gives L.A. its unique character. The landscape will permit anything, all dreams are possible. Identities manifest as simply as a step on the accelerator, an injection of silicone, a brush with celebrity.

The sun-drenched gardens here are as much an expression of fantasy as the buildings or the motion pictures, from the topiary Dumbos at Disneyland to the cypress spires of Mount Olympus. And this surreal and pixilated landscape has made it possible for the quiet, almost unnoticeable existence of wildlife. Where I live in the Hollywood hills I see deer, raccoon, skunk, opossum, owls. And at night I hear the eerie spirituals of coyotes, blues broadcast for the ears of other planets.

The bear, however—whose image parades on our state flag—won't be found lumbering down canyon boulevards in the wee hours, or caught looting in alley trash cans. The bear fled the Los Angeles basin decades ago. So too, the wolf. In their stead are scores of feral cats and dogs, animals fashioned by centuries of civilization, now abandoned to forage in its shadows.

My cat Lucy was a hunter. She resembled Teddy with her tortoise fur, and her eyes like fractured green glass. She brought down a host of small Southern California critters: mourning doves, pigeons, bats, rats, hummingbirds. I'd listen to her teeth crunching bones and be reminded of the saber-toothed cats in the La Brea tar pits. She kept me apprised of the realities of predation. And though I plied her with beef liver from the Mayfair Market (the steer conveniently slaughtered and butchered, the organ wrapped in sparkling polyethylene), she preferred the messy business of hunting. She was also, not coincidentally, a great lover, a generous spirit who taught me unconditional love between individuals of different species. She enjoyed our similarities: liked to lie with stomachs touching, liked to press her pads into my palms, liked to brush her lips against mine. I often prided myself that I'd made sure she was weaned before I took her, sure she'd been schooled well. Kittens, like all young predatory mammals, require the closeness of the maternal bond, through which they imitate the mother's grooming, affection, vigilance and hunting skills. Lucy had learned everything she needed from her mother, both for the kill and for love.

The world of predators is filled with legends of devotion. Stories of mothers, or would-be mothers, or pack mates who give up their lives for those they love. And let's note, in particular, those interspecies love stories: the man who reenters the flames to save the cat, the dolphin who rams the shark to save the woman, the man who fights the other man to save the whale, the wolf who suckles the baby boys.

Predators, it seems, have the knack for love sure as they have the knack for the kill. Aren't those songs of love they yodel to their prey? Even in repose, when it's clear they're off the clock, cats will chatter psalms to a flutter of televised flocks, to the buzz of a fly outside the screen door.

Some human hunters love the animals they kill. They give their prey names before letting the arrows fly, say prayers of thanks when those animals fall. Of course there are scores of more disrespectful hunters, and worse, demonic ones. Richard Chase, the California vampire killer, devoured living birds and smeared his body with the blood of cattle years before he began hunting humans. Each victim was studied like a faceted jewel, each captivated him. Each death was gory, ferocious, intimate. How different is the demonic hunt from the loving one? Both often involve stealth, magical thinking, passion. The line is uncomfortably thin.

Last spring as I was out for a walk in the neighborhood I saw a young buck running down Canyon Drive. The sun caught the golden suede on his new antlers. He was strong, alert and more beautiful than anything I had seen in a long long time. Without even realizing it I had begun to run after him. Within seconds we were joined by a shirtless man, who loped alongside the buck, and who moved with the dangerous, intoxicated gait of a predator. For a moment I feared for the deer, and for the man too, who seemed in such a state of abandon, this half-naked man who ran because something in his blood said "go." Then we all stopped. The deer was rethinking his options, and the man, I realized, had begun to feel foolish. He was in love, clearly, caught up in fascination and the voluptuousness of the chase. But he was a city man. What, after all, would he have done with the buck had he brought him down?

■ ■ ■

There's no way to justify a comparison between a house cat and the god of the forest. It's a tweaked form of anthropomorphism to equate a small pet to a bear, a beast I've never even laid eyes on, except in a zoo. Be that as it may, Lucy is my conduit to the bear's mythos.

And who can blame me? Those immense creatures were chased out of my landscape by guns and traps and the ailing habitat. Who better then than my rapacious cat to show me? Lucy had the requisite features of a flesh eater, eyes close-set for binocular vision, hackles for bluff, and a growl that even I, an upright giantess, had to respect. Then of course she had those glistening canines, the upper left broken off, no doubt by bone. Who better than Lucy to paint the nature of predation—that middle triptych where tenderness and cruelty lay down with each other—my own fierce nature. Who better than Lucy to remind me of bears when, with the night's meat in her gums, her fur smelling of wind, she'd return to curl inside the curve of my belly, to share the safety of our lair.

PET, NOUN & VERB

*: to fondle, caress or stroke. to make love by fondling
or caressing.*

Touching may have been basic syntax to a child, but by
puberty it's the most idiomatic language on the planet. A
comforting pat might translate into a quick feel. A moist-
ening of the lips may falsely signify an invitation to a
schtupping. And even for every correctly perceived come-
hither look, there's a slap in the face. See how torsos are
bound and draped, mouths veiled, how dark glasses
reject entry into the soul? The boundary between public
and private has a different appearance for each culture,
each individual. I may kiss your lips only if we've established a special rapport. And that kiss may last only a
second unless we've established a mutual interest in sex
with each other. We'll seldom trespass unless the welcome mat is out, the attraction, mutual. Even then, the
way I kiss might put you off. Too deep; not deep enough.
Perhaps the kiss itself was fine, but the way I looked into
your eyes at that moment was too much. Touching is
beset with struggles over boundaries, respect and viola-
tion, trust and escape.

Let's imagine for a moment that we leave this hub of
come-ons and mixed messages. It is nighttime and we are
driving out of the city, into the countryside. We turn off
the paved road and drive until this stretch of dirt ends.

Suddenly there they are. Their eyes are a field of stars. We could gaze forever at the constellations of deer, kit fox, skunk and raccoon. But our headlights are their Gestapo siren. So in no time this meadow is swept clean of stars. Deer, fox, skunk and raccoon have all fled beyond the fan of those beams into a neatly sealed dark. The world we came for rejects us by disappearing. Only the stink of skunk remains, insisting we stay put. Respect this distance.

Even on foot, the woods hold back. Crickets hush at the crunch of our approach. The path before us is a scramble of fast exits. We could comb this wood for hours and never see more than the hind quarters of creatures plunging into dark. We're homesick for this world we inhabit but can't touch. And though we try to make ourselves appear harmless, and speak in reassuring voices, we can't hope to lure those critters out by the purity of our intent. We'll be scrutinized behind the safety of distance.

Of course, we've domesticated animals. But more significantly we've formed relationships with them—not simply to do our bidding, but simply to be touched by us. And in being touched they've not only brought themselves beyond their flight distance, they've penetrated our own. Interspecies love stories are the most purely heartfelt, the least conditional. If you don't believe it, compare.

But first before you do, rule out devotion to parents, they are a given, like the color of your irises, the shapes of your toes. Rule out the love of children, who are, after all, a kind of retrieval system, a ticket back to the smooth skin and wide eyes of youth. Rule out the passions governed by the drive to engorge the ego, the grand stuff of opera, the stage strewn with sacrifice, the tragic tenor always hogging the limelight. Rule out even the love of an artist for her art, which is really, dear reader, a thinly veiled ploy for attention, a thickly perfumed valentine to anyone who'll take the time to read it.

Rule out especially sexual love, which occupies so much of our public and private thought. Which, despite the plethora of information about it, repeatedly leads us into unwise couplings, unhappy breakups, and increases in an overstretched population. Of course, sexual love seems colossal, the orchestra is playing full blast and you suddenly discover you move like Fred Astaire.

But soon the honeymoon is over, the orchestra calls it a night, your nakedness is instantly regretful, and the pupils of your Beloved's eyes are a darkness into which frightened creatures are making their getaway. Sex is the predator in you, drawing you into a woods where love eludes you, scrambling for cover.

What joy that pets should claim my home as their lair. They stalk and kill, rub scent onto the corners of my furniture, patrol the yard, and threaten other creatures who trespass. But most of all they stalk my pleasure. With less trepidation than any lover could. And they accept my caresses, show me completely their appreciation of physical love. I know their bodies intimately, and have never felt embarrassed to be naked around them. Of course, you say, they're just animals. This is exactly my point.

THE SMELL OF SKUNK

One summer night a few years ago I was awakened by a wrenching snap. I thought our oak had cracked in half. It was really the night that had been split, razored by light. The gape it left waited to be sealed by thunder. I was already sitting up with my feet on the carpet when the boom finally hit. We were all up: two women, two cats, and a low scuttling shadow in the garden. By the next bolt anyone with a nose could tell who that visitor was, though I couldn't spot him in the strobe of our yard. "He must have found a hiding place," I said to my lover, our bedroom galvanized, her body suddenly incandescent, photoflashed, held freeze-frame en route to the bathroom. The next flare caught her back in bed, complaining about the smell. Indeed, each successive snap and boom, each bright chafe of light made the odor stronger.

That curious earthy stink is not entirely unpleasant. It holds a kind of fascination for us the way uncouth things often do. I imagined it smelled like a sack of rotted chestnuts. A cast-iron cauldron of tar and tobacco. A mongrel jam of sweat and rubber on the insole of gym shoes. Ponderously mammalian, completely pervasive. Like a complex chord played on an old organ—wide awake and all agog.

I began to think our invisible guest had found shelter under the house—his stink now loomed like a formidable ghost. I imagined him crouched in some pocket of clay under the foundation, his nose gleaming with sweat. Fear of this sort is always the drum before the axe, always the body's way of pleading with death. How often had I found myself jolted from the nocturnal forays of my dreams, my heart beating like thunder, the bed steeped in the smell of my own terror? In fear, the skunk and I were twins, equally wild-eyed, both jarred by the same timpani, both ringing with adrenal voltage. In fear we shared the face of our common ancestor, a tiny quasi-mammal, scrambling from under the feet of dinosaurs.

But how far afield our differing ways of coping with fear had led us. Skunks developed a specialized gland near the anus that, used as a last recourse, discharges a noxious odor. Under fire, they resort to chemical warfare, and never against their own kind. Our response to terror is often to take the offensive, to provoke injury, more often than not upon our own kind, and even upon ourselves.

I imagined him out on his nightly route, his journey down the flagstone walks of suburbia, foraging in the garbage, the trash cans crashing like cymbals. What had it been like when that first crack of lightning bleached the garden and made it stick like a burr to the back of his eyes?

What is it like when a flash sears away cover, when havens flatten and fall into bits? When there are no words like *thunderstorm* to glue them back into place? It would be like the image of devastation in my nightmares: a mushroom cloud ushering in the storm—our universe redirected, back to the Bang and then into oblivion. If only my body believed a stink could hold that scene at bay. I grew envious—he would always have his fetid little smell to wage against disaster. But for me, my eyes fixed on the blinking window, annihilation is as inevitable as rain.

■ ■ ■

The skunk lumbers around the periphery of civilization, his fumes disrupting all propriety, a frowzy reminder that nature is accountable to only herself. As we set about at night in our automobiles—the network of concrete muting the landscape, the medians and shoulders sheared and hushed—a stench will drown out our civil quiet, and the word *skunk* will form between us, like a cuss.

Skunk resonates in the Saxon onomatopoeia, as boldly bull's-eyed as *fuck* or *shit*. Something in the nasality relegates skunks to the lumpen class of sense memory. The word is rude and loud. Roll up the window, smooth your lapel.

A skunk is passing through, a tray of Baccarat crystal is dropped, the cerebral cortex is overthrown in the coup, a diaper is run up the flagpole. We sink into the kind of aphasia in which we can only recite obscenities. We are lost to the primitive world of the pheromones.

I am speaking here of chemistry 101. In the realm of sight and sound we are dazzled by the stuff of physics—wave forms, oscillations, vibrations—we're beset by the vaudeville of electromagnetism. But odor is more than show biz—it's the real McCoy. Crack open the oven door and you know the cake is chocolate. Bits of the world drift up for us to sample. The flower sends its delectable valentine, and we're coaxed to its seductive center, gaping into its cunt, its airborne molecules stroking the inner tissues of our nostrils.

Skunks, of course, are sending us eviction notices, walking papers. Stink is indisputable. A noxious smell orders the limbic brain to stay away, and the ancient brain, aboriginal noodle, grunts in compliance.

In the same way it's expert in sex or the wild-eyed ontology of panic, the limbic brain is a scholar of bad smells. A putrid smell marks death and its odious attendant, pestilence. Stench is the skull and crossbones hovering over spoiled food or water. It's the smell of shit—the stuff we have to separate from food if we intend to stay healthy.

Even before the body learns nourishment at the breast, its

survival is a love affair. Amour first flows through the umbilical cord, the insistent pulse of mama's samba is omnipresent, and we know firsthand how communion is Eden. From then on, food, unless you're bingeing, is public domain; we break bread together, the mariachi band will not leave our table, and everyone is ordering dessert.

On the other hand, at the other end, defecation is private. It is the opposite of nourishment, therefore an experience of exile, dispossession. Shit is *from* us, but not *of* us; it must be discarded. Feces represent the release of energy, the breakdown of matter, a body that has been drained of its potential, a corpse that must be given a proper burial. We excuse ourselves from the merriment, waddle to the powder room, and watch our little murders cyclone their way to Davy Jones's locker.

■ ■ ■

My anus, like the inside of my nose, is something I can finger but can't examine. I don't pretend to have a good relationship with it. It is, so to speak, the seat of my unconscious, the organ of my unspoken experience. It alone is witness to the mute pleasures (and pains) visited on me within the sterile receptacle, the private stall.

In the bathroom, Platonic temple wherein matter is transcended and Ty-D-Bol prevails, my turd is a shock that can be instantly and gratefully erased. Each flush conspires in the illusion that no other shit has come before it. The toilet offers no evidence of accumulation, no proof that the body's product constitutes its own body.

The voice of Emerson, of Whitman, of the sixties rises up in me. I want to throw off the chains of the establishment, break through the plastic curtain and squat in the woods. I want at that moment to be saturated in the mineral smells around me, to be surrounded by the decomposing scats of other creatures, to believe the earth is happy to accept my offering.

My body's gifts come painfully and with trepidation. The mouth I cannot see withholds, like a controlling mother. Dark grapes appear around its opening. Each ravage of hemorrhoids leaves my anus ragged, a wilted rose, a mouth pursed in bitter disappointment. I feel shame, don't like to have it touched. It's like the fruit at the bottom of the barrel, split and degenerate.

Mine is a toilet-training success story, a zealot's approach to socialization (like anorexia), an attitude I betray each time I chastise other drivers with the epithet "asshole."

There is a natural affinity between anger and excrement. We sling curses at each other as if, like orangutans, we were hurling our own feces. We say, Shit on you, asshole. It's the bottom line, and we want to rub their noses in it. The limbic brain, again, ready to kick butt, adrenals at full throttle. Poor little Stone Age brain is out of step with the world. We can't seem to manage either our anger or our waste.

The nuclear arsenals accrue, their half-lives outstretching the last human exhalation. The ocean is littered with corroding barrels of poison. There's a fire burning out of control underground, and a hole growing bigger in the sky. How much more warning do we need?

■ ■ ■

I should have seen it coming. Or I should have smelled it coming. Something a little off, a little waft of sulfur, a small slice of cheese. In hindsight it's always easier to ferret out the signs, like rereading a mystery and seeing the foreshadowing bold as day. But at the time I thought our life together smelled like the proverbial rose. The lover whose body was a silver Artemis for a second during a thunderstorm, the woman whose breath smelled of celery, whose armpits smelled of curry—that woman had fallen into the arms of another.

I'm not usually accustomed to showing my anger, but something defensive and primitive elbowed its way to the helm. My thoughts were strictly Neanderthal as I showed her the dark side of my love, and in the wake of the storm my feces were flung.

That was years ago. Last week she dropped by to show me her new van before moving to New Mexico. I've grown accustomed to the changes in her appearance, the transformation from neoconservative to New Ageist—the Birkenstocks, the peace symbol earrings, the crystal of amethyst worn as a medallion.

Yet something about her continues to catch me off guard. There's something alien about her breath, like the inside of a strange car, or hands that have been worrying metal. I tell myself it's probably her new vegetarian diet, or pot. Maybe she always smelled that way and I was too in love to notice. And what about that body odor? The complexities of curry had soured to the funk of burnt onions, scorched fuses, smoldering tires.

■ ■ ■

The skunk, or perhaps a descendant, remains, continuing his nocturnal visits, apprising the neighborhood of his territory. I'm not about to challenge the authority of his message; it rings as clear as Paul Revere's. However sweet and tidy my life may get, however brightly polished the windows, he'll be out there, the perpetual trickster warning, "Watch out!" Or in the vernacular of today's bumper stickers, "Shit happens."

Look, I'm not completely neurotic about excreta. My attitude's not wholly negative. Somewhere deep in the heart of my perineum I recognize shitting as the first experience of movement. Like crying, shitting is a primary and dynamic form of expression. In one of the many myths about Picasso he is asked, "What would you do if you were locked in a room without the materials with which to make art?" He replied, with that characteristic unblinking stare, that he would make art with his own excrement.

Shit is essential *creation*. A series of births, requiring strain, catharsis, and ultimately a sense of pride. Every infant understands this, each envisions her *Demoiselles D'Avignon* smeared in umbra impasto upon the nursery wallpaper. For all that we may vilify poo-poo, we secretly delight in its variety, and in the dumb fact that it is a product of our daily lives. It may be a bit of death, a piece of drek, but it looks like a fish, a jaguar, a totem pole. . . .

My new lover's anus is a finely clenched whorl of flesh. A sealed bud, an unopened chrysanthemum. I've never seen her in a thunderstorm, but I like the way I feel in her arms. Her breath smells faintly of milk, and her armpits smell green, like a stem broken open. Still, some nights I lie tense against her back, waiting for the spooks only my nose can scout. When I find them—no, *if* I find them—they will smell of demolition, of ruptured roadways stretched to impossible distances. They will smell of tar, and the wreck of betrayal.

REVELATION

Though no one in my family went to church, I got the urge in the sixth grade. At each Monday morning recess, B.J. and Mollie had sipped orange drink and talked about their pals at Saint Mary's Sunday school who I didn't know, but of whom I was jealous just the same. An undertow of conformity had begun to swell around me, and along with pixie headbands and madras shifts, Sunday schools and Hebrew schools were suddenly de rigueur. On weekends, instead of thrilling to the beatitudes of my classmates, I was miles away on the sheep ranch my family used as a country home. Though it never would have occurred to me before to complain about being country-bound, I now yearned to be back in The City, carried along by a tide of pious pubescents. And, to be honest, I was also prodded by an unidentified upwelling, a push toward something ecstatic, not unlike the hormonal zeal that was beginning to convert my body. Along with the appearance of my first downy pubic hairs, I found myself weeping over ballads, moonlight, and the meaning of the word *agape*. I was burning to give myself to something, though I couldn't imagine what that something might be. Perhaps, through whatever rites they performed at Saint Mary's, I would.

■ ■ ■

Until then my only religious instruction had come from two sources: the Classic Comic book of the New Testament, and Hollywood's versions of the Old. Both presented wide-angle summaries of the Bible—like oiled Samson, wind-blown Moses, Jesus strolling on a sea of blue Benday dots. I would gape at those American images, not so much from reverence, but more with a prurient interest in the magic, sin and disease they so gloriously depicted. Like my own id, the Technicolor world of the ancients was rife with Bathsheebah, Gomorrah, Mascara.

I longed for a religion with the breadth of Cinemascope, a passion both steamy and elevated, full of special effects. I wanted awe. Wanted to suffer a kind of humility, not like the flagellants, but rather like the child who learns to love a strict teacher.

I had been to Europe as a child, and was instantly mortified by cathedrals. There naked cadavers sagged from walls and people in black whispered to themselves. The smell of frankincense became the smell of wrinkled hands, bleak stones, and vaulting cold. My small voice flew up into the shadows like a lost parakeet.

I thought it was silly to worship a child, perhaps because, being one, I knew that power resided in a realm well beyond the reach of my tiny fingers. The notion, furthermore, that a wiseling could appear ready-made insulted my sense of cause and effect. But worse than the idea of a sage trapped inside the body of a baby was the sight of the crucifixion. Here was a man tacked up like a target, his towel barely concealing his genitals, his conversations with an invisible god a public spectacle. This should have been enough to turn me away from the Gothic excesses of Catholicism, yet I was drawn more steadfastly to it, like Gretel coaxed to the exotic house of gingerbread.

I was smitten with Catholic passion. I had seen this zeal at the movies, as portrayed by Ingrid Bergman and Sophia Loren, amazon martyrs whose scanty robes became scantier through valiant struggle, their revealed shoulders shining like apples, their eyes burning with Catholic lust. I envied that desperate heat in which one became a lioness ready to lay down her life for a cub. That selfless drive was something I could only associate with maternal instinct. And so, at the age of five, in my attempt to classify the natural world by gender, I pronounced my mother Catholic, my father Jewish.

How, except by my process of elimination, did I declare my father to be Jewish? The glory of masochism I had gleaned from crucifixions and sex goddesses—Catholicism was female. But what did I know from Judaism?

I osmosed that from the movies as well, because whenever post-Holocaust Hollywood told the greatest story ever told, testosterone gushed forth like seawater over the Philistines. And even though WASP hunks played the leads, and even though few looked remotely Semitic, given the right angle the chosen could be delivered from Pharaoh. Victor Mature's pectorals gleamed under a Babylonian moon, Charlton Heston's jaws pulsed in the Sinai sunset. As long as each bulge caught a tungsten highlight, Semitic virility stood, as it were, tall in the saddle. Men were Jewish.

My universe then was a grand assembly of dyads, a great Ark into which elephants swaggered and hippos minced. Cows were girls, horses boys. Dogs also were boys, cats girls, and so on, up the evolutionary ladder to Catholics and Jews. Long before I understood the mechanics of reproduction, gender was a conundrum I struggled to clarify, being less certain of how to locate myself among the easily sexed. As a tomboy, wasn't I more dog than cat, more like a river than a lake? What faith would claim me as one of its own?

■ ■ ■

As luck would have it, my family stayed in The City for a few weeks that winter, and I was able to sample the brand of religion Mollie and B.J. endorsed. In a word, Saint Mary's was soothing, with the mild-mannered organ and a placid assembly, each of us tranquilized by rose light and the smell. of White Shoulders. It was a quiet piety, a modest thing, relieved of passion. No pierced flesh, no cups of blood, no ancient languages; it was as harmless as Carter's underwear. Sadly, I was shopping for something more in the way of ecstatic visions, hair shirts and supplication. I grew restless by the third hymn.

What I found in the pews of Saint Mary's was the unction of the Eisenhower era, the cant of McCarthyism. Conformity in lieu of fire. Never before had I seen so many white gloves, so many crossed ankles. "Episcopalian" was apparently something you told people who wanted to know where you fit in, a password into the confident niche of the Protestant upper middle, where one could blend, a trout among trout in a clean tank.

It's no coincidence that my second and last visit to Sunday school involved a field trip to the local synagogue. The modest hymns of Saint Mary's simpered next to the chatter flying around the courtyard of Temple Emmanuel. The very architecture whispered of far-off places; burly Santas sat beside the fountain and deliberated and made me envious. It was a scene from the Moorish period in Spain, the columnar courtyards with their archways, where Jewish scholars rescued the Greek classics from the obscurity of the Dark Ages.

Inside this temple was an even more outstanding thing—at the foot of the assembly, beyond the rows of chairs, perched on a splendid altar—a book where a cross should have been. Here was a religion divested of images, free of focal points where the literal mind might root and grow like a tumor, where symbolic logic reigned supreme and each letter of the alphabet tapered like a flare.

But I wasn't Jewish. I was . . . on my own, separated from

the Talmud by my gene pool, separated from the Holy Mother by the Reformation, and now divorced, by choice, from the claustrophobic restraint of Saint Mary's. The only passion I could claim was an unholy one, one that moved me in dreams, and lifted my prepubescent body toward heaven.

■ ■ ■

Sexuality, not surprisingly, became my denomination, my grail. I was captivated finally, not by the Word or the beacon of Jesus, but by the plastic figurine of a woman. She might as well have been a religious icon, her posture was as guileless as a saint's. She stood without a stitch, Eve before the Fall, her arms outstretched at her sides, her anatomy as disarming as a vision. And even her skin, a clear resin, was committed to further revelation. The Visible Woman was as see-through as an aspirin bottle. Boldly modeling her organs, her divine candor absolved me of guilt—I was free to look, to understand, at long last, what precisely was female. A gift from my mother, the Visible Woman was a graven image for the purpose of inspection rather than worship. She resembled the Visible Man in almost every respect, except one—along with liver, lungs and brain was a womb, also transparent, in which a plastic fetus lay like a lima bean.

This icon saved me in the nick of time, only months before my first menstruation. Not only had the perplexity of gender become a source of shame, but the eroticism of my fantasies had grown more articulate. Spacemen chased me through forests, or breathless teachers pressed my temples to their heaving breasts. Some nights I had a beard, others I was penetrated by a tiger. I had a penis but decided to flush it down the toilet. I would not judge or censor those creations, not only because they roused me, but because, like my feces, they filled me with secret pride. They were formed by my nature.

With spring I saw how life asserted itself on our ranch through all manner of new plants and animals. Like that life, my imaginings were equally protean, eager to assume new guises like children do at Halloween. My delight in fantasy felt as natural as the frisk of lambs, and I knew few religions would condone such heresy.

I studied the Visible Woman's body for months, extracting and inserting the little uterus, imagining a less clumsy procedure whereby a human being would form like a sprout and grow into someone as large as myself. But where did the sprout come from?

I ventured into the illustrations of anatomy books: up into the boiler room of the vagina, with its steel walls shining with steam. I slipped through the os, its smile like the Mona Lisa, and tumbled like an astronaut above the flora of the uterine ecosystem. I was both Lewis and Clark across the span of fallopia, until I marveled at the spongy nurseries, each in turn launching ovum with clockwork coughs. But where did the ovum come from? The mysteries of the nursery were too small to decipher.

I sped to the chapter titled "The Masculine Genital Organs" and dove into the urethra of the penis, into another boiler, where pipes and chimneys ran the length of a tunnel, and the sound of blood pounded on all sides like an ocean. I surfaced into the reservoir of the prostate, where arcs of fluid cascaded above me like the floodgates of Hoover Dam. And finally I penetrated the testicles: each almond was cracked by a cross section, where impossible tangles of spaghetti—four hundred yards of snarled tubules—incubated whole constellations of sperm. But where did the sperm come from? Where did the spark begin?

My questions concerning the spark of life lead me into a realm that was smaller than penises or vaginas, eggs or sperm,

Xs or Ys, a realm made up of twilight particles, spirits who murmur in your ear but can't be swatted away.

I began to see the physical world as the evidence of their mischief—that reality was a mere appearance, like the drapery that defines the body of a ghost. And its spectral anatomy was neither male nor female, human or otherwise, but something beyond classification. Suddenly, my world of plastic organs and anatomy books seemed as flimsy as chintz. It sparkled like the gloss at the ocean's surface, while the real world of gluons and gravitons moaned below like a siren's song.

So there were two worlds: the perceived world, a dimension of adjectives, equations and brush strokes, a surface dazzling with our efforts to render it, but ultimately bearing only our own reflections; and the imperceptible world, the plumbless dark full of latent particles, the primordial cauldron which, like a mother, gives us our being but is a lifelong riddle.

Desire, I realized, was part of the enigma. I sensed that sex, like a strict teacher, demanded surrender; that whatever intimacies I would enjoy in the future exacted the humility I had always craved. And then I saw myself seated before the Visible Woman, longing to know the world I took apart and put back together, knowing I never really would.

DANCING SCHOOLS

Just be yourself," my mother advised as we came to a stop. I maneuvered myself out of the car without showing my underpants or slamming my dress in the car door. Behind the glass of the passenger window she mouthed, "See you at five-thirty," and drove away, down Pacific Street.

Wherever girls congregated in the foyer of the California Club, their petticoats seethed audibly. My crinolines fanned beneath my waist, made my legs look like the clangors of a bell. Below all our puffy bells, beneath our downy legs, we wore thin white cotton socks with scalloped cuffs, and patent leather Mary Janes, each gleaming like a pool of tar. Sugary smells stuck to the air around us, Jean Naté, Wind Song, Daisies Don't Tell. Gloves were requisite wear for girls, and though this regulation seemed absurd to me they managed to conceal my gnawed cuticles from the boys' scrutiny.

It was 1961, Kennedy was still alive, and the Beatles had not yet won our hearts. The standoff at the Bay of Pigs pushed the American psyche closer to Armageddon, and Freedom Riders were heading south. The world was changing in ways I hadn't the inclination or the desire to comprehend.

Mr. Lee announced on the mike that it was time to come into the auditorium. Girls filed in and sat in a long row of chairs to the left, while boys made their way to the row on the right. Squared off, across the expanse of dance floor, many of the boys looked as miserable as I must have. We stared across the room at one another like linebackers, soldiers at the front line, pawns in a game of chess.

Then Mr. Lee announced that it was time for the gentlemen, as he called them, to cross the floor and "ask a lady to dance." This was followed by the sound of a stampede, as the more self-assured boys—all of them tall and more developed—raced one another for a prized girl without breaking into a run. Girls who were unpopular, girls like myself, would try not to appear crest-fallen, our little smiles pasted to our faces, badges of perpetual cheer.

Now knowing how my face always betrays me, I imagine I must have showed my resignation the moment I set foot in the California Club. No boy of eleven could have possibly braved such a distressed damsel.

The less confident boys—the shorter, less athletic ones—always made it to the girls' side of the hall last, and were forced to choose among the wallflowers. This surely must have added to their embarrassment—not only to be left with the dregs, but likewise to be the insult to our injury. Nevertheless, no matter how much resentment one member of the out crowd projected onto another, all of us, creeps and geeks alike, were grateful to be paired finally, standing with the herd.

"Java," a popular song featuring Al Hirt's trumpet, initiated every Monday afternoon like reveille. With each stride, we traced invisible squares on the floor, obedient to this too-friendly tune that could easily have been a jingle for frozen dinners or floor wax.

Mr. and Mrs. Lee were the butt of every joke. Whenever Mr. Lee barked "Change partners!" each boy moved forward to the next waiting girl, and a mantra of remarks concerning the Lees, no matter how hackneyed, forged a bond. "What a fruit," Ricky Pearlstein would mutter under his breath about Mr. Lee, or "God, their taste in music is *so* lame!" Then, with another "Change partners," Charlie Haas would be standing in front of me, mouthing "Fruit" and rolling his eyes, and I would whisper back an *"I know!"* with the same conspiratorial fervor as I had with Ricky.

The blond Mrs. Lee looked desiccated. She barely spoke, never used the mike. Her smile switched to ON the instant her husband placed the stylus on the record, and she waited, arms extended, for him to return from the phonograph and take his place facing her. She stepped briskly backward on heels as tall as her face was long. I swore she was born to be moved like a large, if somewhat sun-leathered, doll. Mr. Lee seemed to possess all the pretense to aristocracy of a butler or an interior decorator. He spoke with a vague English lilt, and struck a course across the dance floor with his jutting chin, giving his wife full view of his nostril hairs.

They moved together as if they shared a sexless intimacy, one single, burning desire only for status; and we, the sons and daughters of The City's elite, were required, we knew, to admire and imitate this affectation. We were alternately compliant with their fantasy and disdainful of it, both their captives and their tormentors.

■ ■ ■

I worry that my right hand is too heavy. He has to hold it up in his left. His thumb presses into my palm. I try to keep my hand suspended so he doesn't have to carry all the weight. My left hand—another dead weight—rests on his right shoulder. I worry that if I don't move it very often, I'll seem frozen, awkward. I adjust the position of my hand ever so slightly so as to appear casual.

We are making squares on the floor with our dance steps. Sometimes he looks down at his feet. His head nods with the beat between steps, and his teeth clamp his lower lip. He is a good six inches shorter than I, and I peer into the part of his hair and see his scalp, white and shiny as candle wax. He smells like Canoe.

■ ■ ■

I am drawn to flowers not only to get a better look at them, but finally to be coaxed inside them. The corolla, the flower's raiment, is designed so that my pupils dilate; and where the eye goes, at least in my species, the nose can not be far behind. So there I am standing at the gape of the calyx, my nose hovering, waiting to sniff. In fragrance I am, like a bug, reduced to primal ambitions, desperate to bury my nose in petals, to plunge my face into crinolines, until my nostrils plumb the source: Jean Naté, Canoe, Chanel No. 5—the musk of the flower's genitalia, mother of all perfume.

With each inhalation I absently stroke the crotch of a hermaphrodite. The stamen, male organ of the flower, is composed of filament and anther. Hinged at the tip of the willowy filament, the anther is poised, eager to seesaw and smear its cornucopia of pollen against anything that comes its way. With a little help from a bee's back, a moth's wing or the end of my nose, pollen may be smooched from the anther to the sticky lips of the stigma, the flower's vulva.

There at the labial threshold the lodged pollen will grow a tentacle, snake down into the flower's ovary, and fertilize an egg.

■ ■ ■

At eleven, two small bulblets—breasts—rose from my chest. I had been warned against roughhousing because I might hit them and then get breast cancer. I was an inveterate tomboy, and wrestling matches aside, everything I did put my new acquisitions in jeopardy. All varieties of small animals, especially kittens, liked to step directly into the soft centers of my chest. Even the still limbs of trees packed a wallop when I'd hoist myself onto them. The books I carried home from school scraped against my nipples with each stride. No undershirt had soft enough cotton.

Every locale of my body broadcast its own alarming message of change. Pimples shone, certificates of bona fide self-consciousness. Downy hair sprouted from crotch and armpits and lower legs. My nakedness, once circumscribed by Carter's underwear, extended now from neck to knees.

I was known as the girl who always wore coats.

Thank heavens for summer. During summer camp I'd be reunited with my body. Like old teammates, my legs clung to the backs of horses and scissored me across lakes. Companionable arms pitched hay or slung manure. My chest worked faithfully to give me breath. At night, slung in my hammock, listening to the calls of owls, I was comrades once more with my faithful, tired flesh.

Farmstead was a down-home, earthy sort of camp, a tomboy's Zion, nothing like the tennis camps to which many of my classmates were hauled. Abe and Eve Crittenden ran the place like a commune, with the philosophy that children, given half a chance, could develop a deep respect for nature and for community. Abe and Eve were the archetypal Father and Mother, the heart and soul of Farmstead's Ark. Abe looked like a bald Charlton Heston. I tried but couldn't imagine his muscular body in anything other than work denims. Eve, outfitted in jeans, cowgirl shirt, serape, and mukluks, her smokey hair braided to the middle of her back, led our morning sing-alongs on her zither. Her eyes urged us to join in with her. And so we did, without an iota of embarrassment or sarcasm.

Saturday nights everyone danced in the barn, and the spice of sweat and soap mingled with grain and tack. Dancers gave of themselves with stomping, whooping panache. With a do-si-do we'd circle our partners, all the while our cheeks were hoisted on smiles. We danced til we were drenched and gasping for air. Old folk danced with young folk, and it seemed like we could bow and reel all the way into fall.

■ ■ ■

Dancing school resumed early in September, a week before school began. My mother dropped me off at the California Club a little late. As I stood in the foyer and scanned the groups of boys and girls I noticed a stillness. Something was terribly wrong. Groups of boys or of girls clustered and looked at me and giggled.

Jeffrey Anne Brophy walked over and informed me that my clothes were passé, that I'd better update my wardrobe, pronto. "The socks," she whispered, "the shoes, . . . you look . . ." —and here she giggled—"like a *little girl!*" Suddenly I could see that yes, the style had shifted; all my classmates looked chic and grown up. They wore form-fitting dresses, their hemlines a full two inches shorter. Their legs looked smooth, hairless and slightly tanned, or was that the shade of their . . . nylons? Nylons suddenly appeared where white cotton socks had been. Pointy flats replaced Mary Janes. Each girl sported some variation of Barbra Streisand hair, sharp, streamlined, urbane. With my prepubescent clothes and a glaring absence of makeup, I was an oversize Shirley Temple. And I knew that, for the next hour and a half, I would be each couple's new conversation piece, a relief from the ritual gripe about the Lees.

The next afternoon my mother and I rushed to I. Magnin. We scoured the racks, barely breathing. By evening I must have shed a dozen or so ill-fitting dresses, each solemn proof that I'd never be able to toe the mark. "We'll find just the right one, don't worry." My mother's voice was meant to reassure, but I thought I could detect a strain of doubt in it. I thought I could hear a suspicion that I was, or rather that we were, somehow odd, out of step. Just before closing, the saleswoman brought in two identical knit empire—(ahm-peer')—dresses, one hot pink, the other turquoise. "These just came in, they're eights, but they run a little large. Maybe they'd work." She hung them on the door. It occurred to me that I wasn't sure whether or not I liked those dresses, but no matter. Taste, a thing I was still to develop, seemed trivial compared to the threat of ridicule. I slipped one on. The material was magic, never wrinkling, reminding me of swimwear. As I studied myself from three angles, each me was neon, Perma-Prest, instantly à la mode, a triptych of contemporary girlhood. Once inside the California Club, wearing one of those bright, high-waisted synthetics, my desolation would go undetected, I would be free to take my place among my peers, as official a female as Jackie or Gidget.

My mother bought both dresses, and we headed for home, worn as victorious soldiers.

Dances at the requisite country clubs began the following year. Real dances with real bands, bands that played "Chances Are" and "Theme from a Summer Place." And though a few songs might have lent themselves to a fox-trot or a cha-cha-cha, most guys resorted to a swaying two-step. Up-tempo songs like "Please, Please Me" or "Louie Louie" allowed us to break contact from each other, to explore the more self-expressive movements of the twist and the mashed potato. It also allowed us the freedom from having to follow or be followed, from having to be appropriately forceful or demure.

The kids in dancing school had all been white, many Jewish. By the time cotillions began many of the Jewish kids suddenly were missing from the dance floor. No Wally, no Rachel, no Joan, no Charlie. I accepted this fact the way one accepts instruction to change homerooms. I felt relieved to be included among the few, like finding a seat in musical chairs. Yet I never once envisioned myself among the winners of that game, a deb at the ball, dancing with my father in a long white dress. For one thing my father, a shy and shiftless millionaire, would have drowned in a room full of men his own age. My father wasn't the type for balls, unless they were highballs, and neither, more importantly, was I. However much I might have resented my father's antisocial behavior, I was nevertheless my father's daughter, ever marginal, barely able to pass.

■ ■ ■

I've come to a remote mesa in Arizona at the invitation of my mother and her second husband, Paul. It's a long dusty hike to get to Walpi, the ancient city. The road is putty colored, the impressions of your soles in the dust are putty colored, and the town, once you reach it, is built in the same putty-colored stone. The sky is a limitless blue, and you can see, from the window of the kitchen where a woman is rolling out a paper-thin pastry called piki, that the world is spread in all directions.

1982 is a good year for non-Natives who want to visit Hopi Land. Most years the ceremonial dances are off limits to voyeurs. This year tourists are allowed to watch, but without the fetishism of cameras. It is April and the dance we've come to see is called the Home Dance.

We wait, standing in doorways for the emergence of the kachinas. For days they've been underground in a kiva, preparing themselves. I try to position myself a few feet away from the rest of my group so as to appear better than the average white Philistine. I'm a feminist anarchist vegetarian who thinks she knows a thing or two about the evils of cultural imperialism, who subscribes to a shamanism-on-the-side, New Age worldview. I am feeling, incorrectly, like I have more in common with these Native Americans than I have with those Eurocentric,

Caucasian capitalists I sheepishly call my parents. But the grim fact is I'm really about as welcome here as Custer, and even my name, BIA, translates into Bureau of Indian Affairs.

The dawn air is biting and the colorful masks worn by the dancers sting my eyes. Only men are dancing, each a member of a clan. Their movements are rhythmic and monotonous. The bells on their ankles jangle with each successive hop and stomp, as do their droning voices. The man at the head of the snaking line yells and tosses some cornmeal at my feet.

Normally, with my ultra-feminist ideology I'd be piqued by an all-male, somewhat martial, dance. But my arrogance is flattened by the peaceable intent of the dancers. The precision of each step guarantees the continuation of nature's productivity. The exactitude of this army's movements ensures the universe is made right, year after year.

I wish my father had been able to be a member of a clan, not a Hopi clan of course, not a Badger, Spider or Snake clan, but a member of something potentially his, the Gillette clan, the Brittany Spaniel clan, the Mushroom Gathering clan. I wish he'd been able to perform an indispensable movement, to step with his community into a future.

And to whose clan do I belong? I worry about my future on the plane from Phoenix back to L.A. About what, and who, is home.

■ ■ ■

The music is blaring when we reach the top of the stairs. The bouncer runs a metal detector down our legs, the cashier stamps a purple blur on our hands, and we move en masse down a hallway, a school of fish surging through a dark channel.

Every conceivable expression of gender, every possible hybrid of ethnicity moves with us. The Aztec Spaniard is getting down with a Viking. Celtic freckles brush up against African aubergine. Korean wants to mix it up with Persian, East Indian with Ashkenazi Jew. Some younger women look like vampires, others like newscasters, others still, sumo wrestlers. Older women, like myself, still persist with last decade's dull androgyny. Some guys, whether muscled or not, sport makeup and marabou. Even some heterosexuals are here, peppering the stew. The only constants among these throngs are piercings— one earlobe at least—and a burning, yearning desire to dance.

This had been a difficult evening to negotiate: she was considerably younger, but of more concern, she had never been with a woman. She would probably expect me, the older, more experienced, to take the initiative. On the other hand, if aggressive, I might scare her off.

Mutual friends offered a strategy. It had been decided the date should be camouflaged. I would ask her out by simply saying "A group of us is going dancing, would you like to join us?" My friends would accompany us, then make themselves scarce.

So finally the human river deposits us at the front of a vast dance floor. The lights are surging over us. Sweat glazes the cheeks, necks, and (sometimes bare) chests of countless bodies. With a new song our friends, my camouflage, disappear as planned, and she and I are left standing with only each other and two hundred or more gyrating strangers. The beat is at once a distraction and reminder of the space between us. Her eyes sparkle over the dancing hordes, and her knees and hips echo their movements. Do you want to dance, I venture. Her yes brims.

It's been a while since I've danced, I'm rusty and encumbered by shyness. I know how soon the music will melt awkwardness away, how my spine will become a conduit for rhythm. I am starting to feel the thaw of confidence when she moves toward me. I'd hoped for this moment but, dear Jesus, so soon? I am supposed to be the older one, the wiser one, remember? The one who's been here before, so what does she think she's doing, anyway? Susan's hands clasp the back of my neck and her face shines up to me like the surface of a lake.

■ ■ ■

Needlefish glimmer against the water's underbelly like the chimes of steel guitars. Meanwhile, parrot fish the size of watermelons sail below us, blowing us kisses with full kahuna lips. Susan is in her element. Once she gets the feel of breathing through the snorkel she takes to the water like a . . . well, not a fish, more like a beaver, a sleek mammal with a purpose.

Plumeria grow as tall as trees in the Hawaiian Islands, and by twilight their odor sweetens the trade winds. We're worn from our day in the sea, and position ourselves, mai tais in hand, in the hotel lanai, as close as possible to the hula dancer. Each movement of her hands, feet and hips expresses the temperature and heft of the breeze, the upwelling of the tides. But it's the movement of her eyes that makes the dance come alive, as if she sees and delights in each flower and raindrop her hands describe. Her eyes radiate. Susan says the dancer is channeling something holy, an Hawaiian Divinity.

Out in the ocean, in the bluing water, the fauna are mating, bodies are in thrall with one another. I think of the ardent embrace of one octopus upon the other: sixteen tentacles clasping their summary of flesh, their mouths pressed into a kiss as inescapable as a black hole. Their eggs careen toward each other, hopelessly in love. Meanwhile, out in the shoals of the mainland, the bisexual oyster is laboriously sucking in or spewing out sperm to suit the gender of its suitor—its life is a testament to the strong-arm tactics of attraction. And even when it's served up on a plate, its last moments will be spent in the service of desire—that we may remember the ocean's musk, the taste of salt, the moon asserting her charms in the salacious rocking of the tide. And then there's that moon. What brings her to our window night after night if not lust? If not the howling of our planet, our tides straining to win her gasp. And farther out, up in the yawning dark, all of the many bits of the universe are drawn together, goo-goo-eyed, dancing like this was the first night of a honeymoon.

A bird wakes us at dawn, an Hawaiian myna I think. I hear in his mischief the familiar timbre of my backyard mockingbird. He swoops to a spot in the hibiscus bush below our window. With the dawn's light its five-petaled flowers rotate open like slow-mo whirligigs. The red skirts slowly cyclone until they are shamelessly splayed, the sex now free-standing, eager. Both female and male, stigma and anther are of one construct, one hopeful expression. These genitals sway above their red sarongs, waiting for the likes of me to pass by.

Later, on my way to the ocean, I brush against the hibiscus and transport pollen as innocently as a bee, gold smeared against my hair, streaked along my shoulder.

■ ■ ■

The room is dimly lit, as though by torchlight, but you can see Tiki gods grimacing from every post, lamp and goblet. Kelbo's is an ersatz Polynesian watering hole, a cartoon vision of primitive paradise, an L.A. spot for the nearly geriatric and the very gay. We are munching on pu-pus and sucking up drinks through two-foot straws, taking in the atmosphere, toasting our host, whose birthday we're here to celebrate.

Susan and I are the only women at our table. A handsome doctor tells a story about an experiment in which centrifugal force has squeezed babies out of pregnant women. Several guys laugh. It's a kitsch environment, kitsch evening, and I suppose, kitsch humor. But Susan and I are horrified that this would be remotely amusing to some of our friends. Our eyes lock, our jaws set. To me it seems a little like laughing during a lynching, finding humor in the way the corpse had shit his pants. I mention that the story is mean-spirited, and hold my breath. Gratefully Robert, who also is not laughing, uses the dreaded word *misogyny*, saving me from having to be the feminist in the punch bowl. Too late, I can tell the doctor has been made to feel embarrassed by my comment. He and his lover avoid me for the rest of the dinner.

As soon as the jukebox starts up all is forgiven, Benny Goodman has coaxed us away from the table, and Susan and I are desirable quantities once more in this company of bachelors. Male and female, we are each for the other the means to pass onto the dance floor, tickets to the hetero E ride. Where gay laughter may have dominated Kelbo's dining room, the dance floor is clearly the roost of the older heterosexual clientele.

Dancing with Robert, our bellies brush each other. We are middle-aged veterans of most of the baby boomer wars: the generational wars, the hallucinogens wars, the antiwar wars, the civil rights wars, the gender wars, the sexuality wars, the wars-within-our-own-camp wars. He swings me out and reels me back in. Swing, in fact, is the name of the dance we're doing. I feel like a Duncan yo-yo. We are twirling and whirling, and the dance steps of thirty years ago come back, easily, gratefully. We are sweating, damp, working our way toward exhaustion.

Robert smells like some spicy Italian cologne I can't identify. Older Jewish couples are smiling at us, mistaking our momentary joy for a happy marriage. I look across the room at Susan—my true spouse, my associate in the Bread Maker clan, the Snorkeling Beaver clan, the Pollen Envoy clan—and wink as I spin out one more time.

BATS

for Susan

The bed is too large. The sheets extend from my feet like a lip of an iceberg. Leagues beyond the cliffs of my bed is the freezing floor, a tundra where grotesques writhe in the dark like the souls in a Bosch purgatory. One figure always emerges from that swarm and steps into the center of my room. He wants to drain my body of its life by seducing me. And I know I will be powerless to stop him, as powerless as I am to keep my body from sleep, from sex, or even someday from death. And because I am unable to control my body or my life I am terrified.

It is 1962 and I will soon be twelve years old. Thus far I have lived in fear of little but this vampire mythology. My father drinks, my parents fight, the bleak house trembles, but I fear only Dracula. In these olden days, the story of Dracula is a bedtime waking nightmare, a drama in which I stockade myself against the dark powers of annihilation. All children are fundamentalists, and every cell in my body is zealous to win the fight against the night, my small ego trying to sustain itself against the forces I can not name.

In 1962 my parents travel through the Mediterranean. They are in their midforties, and looking back on it, I'm sure they were trying to rekindle the romance in their troubled marriage. Under the lax supervision of my grand-mother, I spend hours alone in the woods.

One day I explore an old shack, a derelict chicken coop. The timbers are weathered to a pewter, and lichen, as finely laced as antimacassars, have grafted themselves to the siding. At first glance there is little inside to sustain my intrigue, some ancient straw and a few daddy longlegs. Then I notice something furry in a crack near the door jamb. I poke it with my finger but nothing happens. I poke again. This time a small claw strikes back, calling my bluff. I feel silly to be reprimanded by such a small creature, but I don't push my luck. Though I've never seen one before, there's no mistaking it's a bat.

The little foot shredding the air between us has permanently marred the membrane between the real and the make-believe. From that day forward I try to strike a compromise between the tiny creature in the door jamb and the emblem of my dread.

■ ■ ■

I'm now as old as my parents were in 1962. I look at their worn passport pictures and see them both reflected in my mirror. As a child it took forever for their likenesses to float up to the surface of my reflection. Then I'd scour my image for their traits, hoping to recognize the hybrid confluence of genes, as if some taproot plumbed the strata of my predecessors and could ground me, securely in myself. Now my face seems haunted by expressions from which I'd give anything to be cut free—mother's resignation, father's trap-door pout.

Blessedly there is also mystery in my face, a dark physics (the closer you get the more it eludes you), a void at the gate of the pupil, a peephole to the great by and by. This is what keeps me glued to the mercurial glass, a hint of something foreign about me. The faces of bats are a little like that, a little like missing the last step of a staircase, a little like falling in love.

Bats' ugliness is appealing, the way a lover's least attractive feature can fill you with hopeless lust. Their nostrils blossom into radar dishes, heraldic bracts more suited to the armature of beetles. Here's a guy about the size of a hamster. His ears resemble the translucent leaves at the core of a head of romaine. He's got two little smokestacks coming out of his nostrils and a set of pearly whites as friendly as pinking shears. Another guy's got the ace of spades for a nose, and a lower lip like a drip of pink frosting. Here's a face like magnified spore, another like genitals that have been under water too long.

Sometimes, love, when your face is transformed by thoughts I can't imagine, you look as alien. The depth of your pupil is as plumbless as a Mesozoic night. The cave of your mouth is as foreboding as a crypt. This is the nightmare I will reach for in your arms, a grotto offering shade from the relentless glare of me. Your cape will graze my face, I'll surrender to the drug of you, trust death enough to free-fall breathless back to our bed.

■ ■ ■

There was a time when all mammals shared a common face, the jittery, bug-eyed kisser of a marsupial shrew. A time before the dim winter choked the sky with dust, and the last elephantine lizards grew torpid and fell. But once the cold stiffened those flat feet, and the thunder through the marshlands stilled, the hirsute shrew multiplied, and the age of warm-bloodeds began.

The waters of the New World teemed with turtles and crocodiles, the modified reptiles, but we'd be hard-pressed to spot our kin among the creatures we'd find there. Elephants looked like warthogs; dogs, arboreal weasels. We were small as lemurs, still clinging to branches, relying on our sense of smell. Bats, however, were sprinters on the evolutionary track and soon looked remarkably like themselves. While our limbs took painstaking millennia to grow beyond a childhood of rodentia, their fingers already extended, Nosferatu-like, to support the opened umbrella of their wings. Some varieties of bats sprouted elaborate nose florets, instruments for the broadcasting of ultrasonic signals, and fantastic ears to retrieve those signals once they'd ricocheted. These were sophisticated creatures who navigated vast distances and pollinated the new flora of the ancient world, who knew the Earth eons before we were able to snapshot it with history. They were skimming the rising mists for airborne insects, sowing seeds with their guano, leaving their fossil remains among thousands of now-outmoded species. They watched as deserts expanded, glaciers retreated, oceans swelled or shriveled.

No wonder we fear them. In the presence of bats we sense the occurrence of time before us. In their impossible faces we see a life that eludes us, centuries of caves, forests of unfamiliar trees, Edens buried under rubble. We are like Nabokov's friend who, upon seeing a home movie taken before his birth, realized to his horror "he did not exist there at all and that nobody mourned his absence."

Bats have always done their business while we're prone, unconscious, our worlds oblivious to one another. While our hands languish and our eyes close and we fly into our dreams, their hands fan open to support the drapery of flight. A skin as thin as an eyelid is stretched across the flare of their spidery finger bones. The umbrella opens and they're airborne, departing for God knows where at dusk, returning at dawn.

■ ■ ■

For both species hands were everything. Ours evolved into grasping tools, digits wise enough to fasten a suture, articulate a prelude or wipe away a tear. The world we've fashioned waits for the touch of our fingertips. In the ever-quickening loop of hand-eye coordination, buttons await our desires like dutiful genies. "Push us," they flirt, peppering America's kitchens, a domino at the door of each elevator, a regimen thousands of feet below ground in a room that may someday launch the big one.

This braid of synapses between hand and eye has enabled us to construct information. With the buildup of the written word we construct a memory outside the body. Now our evolution takes place in our handiwork. The limestone chambers, embellished with stalactites, soot-smudged and hand painted, vault into cathedrals and postmodern archways. With a thumb for a rudder, we cruise the galaxy of television stations at warp speed.

This accretion of gadgetry is something we call progress. Yet while our culture becomes increasingly ocular, our fear of darkness grows more acute. Inwardly, behind the glare of glass buildings, beneath the hum of hard drives, is the same fierce stooge, protagonist of human history, a coward in the dark.

Night is rapture for bats. The midbrain of the bat—the hearing center—is highly developed, their ears survey realms that are inaccessible to us. Songs are cast like nets, to ensnare dazzling nightscapes. Something in their high-pitched chatter enables them to negotiate the traffic inside their swarming black cities, allowing them the most elevated form of anarchy.

What does a bat hear as it flies over my city? The sighs of the crestfallen, the rattle of dice, the chatter of countless deals? And what would music look like to them—a mirage, a distracting collection of motes, an hallucination? The basso rondos of toads, the rosin scherzo of nightingales—would the whole paean of night swirl and glow like a painting by Turner? And layer onto this picture the polyphony that soars at a register beyond our knowing—the ultrasonic arpeggios of lovesick moths, the madrigals of countless insects—how would each sound fit into the picture within the midbrain of our bat?

■ ■ ■

Each spring about twenty million female Mexican free-tailed bats migrate to the Texas hill country, where they stay through summer to bear and raise their young. My friend and I have traveled to a maternity cave reputed to be one of the largest in North America, from which, each night, six million of those hungry females forage the Texan air, devouring forty-five tons of insects.

When we arrive we find a small crowd of people already assembled outside the entrance to the cave. Folks in lawn chairs fish beer out of coolers. A flock of ten-year-old girls scratch bites on their bare legs and whine about the stench of guano. It is well after sundown but not quite night: time for the bats to emerge. Finally a few brave the human chatter and flutter out, followed in no time by a steady torrent of thousands. Their bodies swarming against the dusk look like wavelets on the surface of a flood.

Soon all daylight is gone, and with only the moon to glaze the surge, the crowd of people disperses. We stay, watching the shadows of bats flicker against the moon-blue ground. We feel the breath of their wings against us, and hear the sound of their climb. My friend says it reminds her of rainfall. I think, fire. The bats are still pouring out when we leave an hour and a half later.

Later that night my thoughts purr with Lugosi's Transylvanian accent, "Children of the night—what music they make!" I understand why these creatures embody the supernatural. Darkness blossoms as they soar out, withers as they swoop back. They are envoys of the mysteries of night. The Chinese, romancers of dualism, know how yin cradles the yang, and regard the bat as a harbinger of good luck. But for Westerners, bats wear the black cape of civilization. Sardined in their murky cities, a marvel of packaging, bats are like executives in the sleeping capsules of those Japanese hotels. Or the people we read about who thrive in the brutal subterranea of Manhattan, citizens of the Other, obeying unimaginable laws. We give our gods to the mirror; our monsters to the bat.

I imagine a time before this antagonism was possible. I crawl back up the branches of the evolutionary tree to the last point at which our DNA matched the bat. There both species inhabited the body of an animal like a tarsier, with eyes like nothing a Keane painting could touch, mobile radar-like ears, and a newfangled phallus. The structure of the penis would become a unique feature shared by bats and higher primates—the gorillas, the chimps and the painters of Lascaux. From that point forward we would be cousins in the clan *corpora cavernosa*—possessing cylinders of spongy tissue that fill with blood during sexual excitation—and *corpus spongiosum*—serving to facilitate the erection of the penial head. Among bats even the foreskin would become erect, after intromission, causing the amorous creatures to be locked in coitus.

Like us, bats are sexy and long-lived. Of course, I'd already cast my vote with the Chinese—with the hordes of bugs bats nab, the scores of plants they pollinate, their neighbors would be lucky indeed.

Later still, hoping to catch their return to the cave, my friend and I drive bleary-eyed back out to the site. We park our car at the foot of the trail and climb toward the entrance. It's an hour before daybreak, the moon has fallen, and only a few stars gleam like bubbles in the ink. As we approach the cave we hear something like the ocean. My friend exclaims they're all around us, but I can't see them. I feel the wind of them again, though stronger this time, and occasionally I'm pelted by the residuals of their night's feeding. Their wings thrum like small kites as they plummet back toward the cave. And layer onto this, love, the squeals from inside their city, a few million expectant bats readying themselves for bed.

I can see them better now. A blur of new arrivals is spooling into a cyclone within the bowl of the cave—a holding pattern before they rise to rest. My thoughts keep circling back to you as I stand at their threshold—I'm thinking of a shadowy place only you and I can go. The smell of our rut is the only fragile evidence we carry back to the light of day.

Dawn is eking in, a smudge of zinc. I peer up into the dim morning and see a funnel of them, hundreds of feet in altitude, its spout draining around me. I stand in their current like a ghost, impervious to impact. Gradually the sound of the ocean recedes. With each increment of light there are less of them, until finally, the light has gone golden, a bird sings, and the last few stragglers career back in.

■ ■ ■

Let's say it's night and I've just reread this essay. I set it down on my desk, leaving my trusted circle of lamplight. I close the door on all that is warm and known to me. The dark wall that pushes me back is Cocteau's mirror, the door to the Underworld, and I cast myself into it. The breadth of the night unfolds in leagues until I am a tiny fish gliding in its sea.

■ ■ ■

One morning in 1962 after my parents have returned from their trip, I enter their bedroom to have my mother sign my blue books. She's disappeared from her half of the bed, but my father, propped on his elbow, volunteers his signature. I reach across the bed and offer up my exams, which are the color of robins' eggs. And as he autographs them and I smell the spice of his skin, I notice my mother's form concealed under the covers behind him.

Later that day I'm sent home from school with my first menstrual cramps. I lie in bed and savor my morning's discovery— the only time I ever suspected my parents of having sex—and study the present they've brought me from their travels. It's a piece of rock from the crypt of a sleeping pharaoh.

The pharaoh is wrapped for the deepest slumber imaginable. Mythology says when he finally wakes he will fly out of his stone tomb and into the night. The world will be changed by the centuries. Great rivers will be diverted. Cities will cast their own starlight. This phantom will soar long after that light is dimmed, long after the cities are buried by rubble.

Recently I was sitting with my mother in the house she has shared for twenty years with a new husband I've come to think of as a father. We rest our feet among piles of magazines on a small wooden coffee table. It's the oldest thing in this house that bears the stamp of my history. I remember the sour taste of its varnish, how my four-year-old tongue once traced the carved bodies that ran on all sides. I'd always thought they were the bodies of flying men, or dogs in capes. "Are those *bats*?" I ask her.

"Yes, it's the first piece of furniture your father and I ever bought. We were living in a little flat in Chinatown. The Chinese believe bats bring happiness."

I imagined my parents then, smooth skinned, thinner, little to live on but love. Their room is furnished with the donations of well-wishing relatives, a hooked rug, mismatched chairs, a creaky four-poster. I can't help thinking my mother likes being on top, that in those young days their sex is playful, their smell mingling with the smoke and ginger of the street. Near the bed, at the center of their new lives is the table, bought for hope and a toss at the future. The bats draw back the seam of night, like coverlets for my parents to fall into, and sew that seam back up at dawn, like the last good-luck kiss before rising for work. These lovers are strangers to me, unparents, animals not yet flexing around the beginning of my life. Their cells mingle hundreds of times before a fluke will yank me from the Void.

BLOOD

Fe, fi, fo, fum . . .

Start with the ocean. That primordial stew once served as the blood supply for all the world's life. Single-celled organisms wobbled through Eden absorbing the feast that bathed them, much as the cells of our tissues are served by the blood in our bodies. The soluble realm delivered the goods, then swept the wastes away.

Let's stand on some promontory, say on a cliff in California, the Pacific lifting its skirts below us, and contemplate this intimacy, how the ocean came to live inside us. The salty bouillon is still teeming with minute flora and fauna—protozoa, algae, bacteria—but more complex life has evolved here as well. Some cells have clustered together, forming larger bodies.

A kelp forest undulates in the tides. Its khaki spatulate leaves, a vast surface area, allow the maximum number of cells to access the ocean. They gobble its CO_2, its filtered sunlight, and sigh great sighs of oxygen.

Below these forests is the abalone. A community of cells has formed a pearlescent rampart around the cells of its softer interior. Marine water is pumped through holes in the shell, through tubes, and circulates around the tender mass. The abalone feeds and breathes. The ocean water, now carrying waste and respired water, is expelled through the holes in the shell.

After snatching the abalone from the bottom, the otter reclines atop the ocean's surface as though slung in a hammock, cache of abalone riding her paunch. She is a piece of work, more complex than either abalone or kelp, a megalopolis of specialized cells.

The cells of her stomach, for example, conspire in the industry of digestion, each doing its part to dissolve the gobbled abalone. These chemists, waste management specialists, architects of elasticity, are so specialized, so localized within her body, they can no longer reach the ocean, much less feed easily from it. So the fluid realm is housed within, blood circulates to all points of the megalopolis, the citizens of the body are nourished within a branching network of veins, the cells of the otter's stomach sample the abalone, at long last. With a little sigh, the otter, bobbing on the blue-gray water, closes her eyes and licks her lips.

Looking over the Pacific, the great kelp branches roll into curlicues, each whorl like a Mandelbrot set. The enormous pulse of the surf is a lullaby my satchel of blood remembers.

I once rode in an amniotic sea. Fluid cushioned me and a great blue vein tethered my belly to something larger than myself. Though dimly, I can almost see my growing shape, a curled tadpole preparing itself for a life to be lived on land. I carry the precious fluid within now. God help me if I ever lose my five quarts.

■ ■ ■

My father could trace some of his bloodlines across the ocean to England, a heritage he played to the hilt, a fantasy of landed gentry, with his brood of hunting dogs, his collection of guns, a fondness for organ meats and hard liquor.

In the rumpus room, where I would escape afternoons to listen to records, a rack of antique rifles stuck out like a haunted galleon. Crowning that rack lay his heirloom, an enormous elephant gun, his father's before him, its gaping barrel wide enough for shooting softballs. Those old guns were trophies, not tools, but in the living room, where I watched "Gunsmoke," "Combat" and "Father Knows Best" on weekends, my father displayed his hunting guns. Inside the glass case each shotgun stood oiled and upright, snug in a recess of felt. A few boxes of shells were stacked in readiness on the bottom. But more commanding than these guns was the secret one, one that was neither for hunting nor for show, the pistol he kept upstairs in a drawer with his handkerchiefs and boxer shorts, its metal rod clean and cold against cotton.

The phallic implications of his arsenal were not lost on me, a young teenager. He was trying to erect, with the props at his disposal, a façade of potency. Inheritance had allowed him to retire young. With no job, no direction, no self-esteem, he withdrew into himself. On weekdays he wore down the threads of his armchair. The books he read seemed to absorb him, though he spoke of them to no one, not even my mother. On weekends he walked in the country, hunted, or gardened. He had painfully few words for us, though when he watched football on TV he swore at the set like a coach on the sidelines. As he got older his breathing got louder, each exhalation grunting in his throat. With strangers he grinned like a frightened animal. He was, to put it mildly, ill at ease.

For this reason he drank. Had he succeeded in his vision of maleness—had he been, say, a lumberjack, a senator or a linebacker—he might have drunk anyway. Drink was in his blood. He drank like his father before him. Wine with dinner, beer with lunch, and strong coffee, brief antidote, for breakfast. But most of all it was Early Times, one quart of it, with water, on the rocks, starting at noon, all day long. Four quarts of fluids a day. Glug, glug, glug.

Even before statisticians revealed the genetic nature of alcoholism, I knew at a young age that alcohol would claim a chunk of my legacy. How could a child of a drunk not know this? My ears were as keen as a superhero's to the tinkle of ice from downstairs, piqued to a slower, heavier kind of footfall, tuned to the thickening of mucus in his growling throat. My nose was like a bloodhound's for the vapors of uncorked booze, for the breath that smelled both honeyed and dangerous. My vision could penetrate walls and calibrate the downward slope of his scowl, the milliliters remaining at the bottom of his bottle. I genuflected to that bottle, a zealot awaiting her day of judgment.

How could I not? How could a child of a drunk escape the dread when, say at Thanksgiving, a swallow of wine burned like VapoRub inside her chest, and whet her tongue for a stuporous world? How could she not reach for the bourbon sepulchre in hopes of stealing the family throne?

For ten years I drank, like my father, like a lush. I was proud of how much I could hold, of how well I could drive, of how quickly and cleanly I could vomit in someone else's home. Now I thank my asthma for putting on the brakes, for imposing a minimum, for saving me from speeding into the void.

I love to drink, not only blood red wine, but great quantities of fluids. Juices, teas, coffee, milk, waters. Washed down iced or steamed, fizzy or flat, with lemon or without, at room temperature or sucked from a frozen mass. I like to gulp drinks fast, I like to swallow hard. I like carbonation to burn my throat, to gulp in succession until I belch. I like to stick my nose deep inside the bell of a glass, to smell the nuttiness of an espresso, the rosiness of a Gewürztraminer, the nip of ginger ale. I drink fluids as though I were in the grips of continual thirst. I drink like my father, like a fish.

Don't get me wrong, every time I hold a glass of anything

over 2 percent, I know I'm gambling. Wicked Bacchus is at one ear. The Bacchus I envision is Caravaggio's, coy, half-naked, offering up the goblet of sensation. "It's your own blood, your own life. Taste. *Live!*"

At the other ear is Carry A. Nation pointing to the rotted corpse of my father. "It's his blood," she scolds, "don't fool with genetics." I'm four times more likely to unlock that crypt and crawl inside with my father, and so I listen as I cautiously sip, this time with an inner ear, for the sound of growling in my veins.

■ ■ ■

Liver was once believed to be the seat of the soul. Jesus was speared there, Prometheus gnawed there, oracles saw the future opening in its pores. Alcoholics, protagonists in their own right, blow up there. If alcoholism is indeed a spiritual disorder, a need to consume the spirits missing inside, then the liver is its target, inflating like self-importance. Liver, filter of toxins, is the seat of the ego.

Booze is a kind of essence. A hothouse of roses condenses into droplets inside a beaker, so too, moonshine, nose paint, mountain dew. Dionysus rises like a genie from the oak barrel, the corn still, the hop kiln. We drink spirits and are in turn possessed by them. Like children who spin themselves dizzy for the sheer joy of it, we need to be spun from this world, need our vision to be skewed.

There are some substances which, by the nature of their transformation, by the virtue of becoming a greater whole than the sum of their parts, are magical. Honey, for one. The reproductive juices of sage, distilled by the barfing of a few thousand bees, turn into honey. Silver brambles alchemize into sunlit fructose. Minute yeasts belch CO_2 into pockets of gluten, and the loaves rise. Or they fart into a mash of crushed grapes and after a decade the Brunello yields unexpected flavors, chocolate, black currants, thyme. This is alchemy of the least esoteric sort. One class of substance transforming into another, gas and all. Cud into Camembert. Tubers into seventy proof.

If only our blood could be like wine. Grapes into ruby port. Lead into gold. Flesh into god.

■ ■ ■

As I write this I am bleeding. I haven't been punctured, cut, torn or bruised. This isn't the sort of bleeding that causes panic. It's that here-we-go-again kind of bleeding, the monthly sacrifice-to-the-moon kind of bleeding, a would-be mother's innards proffering potential life. I'm on the rag, got the curse, riding the cotton pony. This blood's cycle, like the ocean's tides, swells and ebbs every twenty-eight days.

Menstruation begins timidly. Squeeze a smudge of burnt sienna from the tube, rub it on a clean cotton pad. In a few hours add a little alizarin crimson. By the next day pour in a quart of cochineal. After two days reverse the process. Then, poof, clean sheet of canvas til next time.

In general, menstrual blood has more viscosity than regular blood. Then there are the occasional claret globs, the clots that, as they squeeze through the os, wrench the gut more than coffee ever could.

Perhaps these details are unsavory, but isn't this my point? Blood is our most private terror, our most intimate fascination. Who among us is not held spellbound by its beacon? The bright bubble that rises when a scab is wrenched away?

Children are most intimate with scabs, most shameless in their love of gore. The knees and elbows of my tomboy days were patched with brown polka dots; I examined them with the fervor of a chimp grooming its kin. Up close scabs looked like jerky. Sometimes, especially on my knees, scabs looked like an aggregate of fudgy granules, a dark mosaic held together in a fabric of dry filaments.

Picking scabs was a lesson in patience. When they were ready, edges gave easily, lifted to a newer skin. But when they weren't, when the lid was pried open too soon and red boiled out, I pressed the scab back, hoping blood would paste the lid shut. Sometimes I preferred to tear it off anyway, to suck up the blood, my lips puckered around the spot like a leach. Blood tasted like butter cooked in an iron skillet.

A few years ago I had my wisdom teeth pulled. During the procedure, which seemed to last hours and involved a hammer, a chisel, and more hands than I thought I could accommodate, I started to bleed. The warm, slightly viscous drops tapped a rhythm in the back of my mouth and comforted me, welcomed me into my body. And when I spit into the porcelain basin, the taste of salt and iron was a rapture as deep as masturbation.

■ ■ ■

Staccato here. My memories are fast and sharp. I was sixteen, away at boarding school. I had been up since five, playing soccer in the rain. My clothes were slick with mud. The vice principal came up to me at breakfast and asked me to follow him into his office. His face was drawn and he fell silent as we walked down the hall. All I could think was that someone in the dorm had ratted on me for smoking. "Boy, it sure must be bad," I offered, smiling, hoping to defuse the reprimand sure to come.

My brothers stood up as we walked into the office. It must be real bad, I said to myself, though I already knew. Their pained expressions, the thunder of my father's rages, his empty bottles of Early Times, the Colt among his underwear.

The whole drive home I kept asking them why, as if I didn't know, as if I hadn't always known. Peter offered, "Sometimes people get themselves into the grip of a vise, and they don't know a way out." He spoke those words as though he had memorized them long before and had saved them just for that moment.

Mother said she had heard a sound like a door slamming, then thought, no, not a door, something else. When she opened the door she saw him slumped, a streak of red on the wall, a second of red, a blur of something red and she quickly closed the door. By the time I got home the blood was gone, rubbed away, only a hole that tore the fabric of wallpaper in a corner of the ceiling. Had he tasted the barrel? Did he close his eyes? Had bits of his head, like Kennedy's, been torn off? How many hours did it take to scrub away the evidence? How long had my mother paced while I was away sleeping or playing soccer in the mud?

Away at school I had been free, not the sleep-deprived sentry of my household, the watchdog chained to the liquor cabinet. Away at school I was no longer a scholar of thuds and shattering glass. Over cold scrambled eggs I said, "I was mean to Daddy, I should have been nicer." I had, in fact, steeled myself against him. Opaque as glacial ice. Richard countered, "So? He was mean to you too." His response fit, though it, too, seemed rehearsed for this moment, a reply saved for his own moments of doubt.

Guilt continues with me, as it did when he was living, a stain I can't seem to wash away.

■ ■ ■

A garnet drop, a pomegranate seed, a pool of horror. A badge of courage, a declaration of war, a plastic bag suspended above the body.

History runs inside it. It screams for justice, challenges detergents, points the finger. Shed without mercy, it can run in the streets, seek its own vengeance. Contracts with the devil are signed in it. It's a vampire's rhapsody. A mosquito's empire. A person can develop the taste for it. It is thicker than water. It carries the virus.

A ruthless thirst. It can be found on one's hands, on the saddle, in a bank. Virile when red, upper crust when blue. An excitable ingredient, made to boil or curdle, run hot or cold.

A fellow, a black male, an L.A. gang. It is paired with thunder. It can mingle and make its own bonds. A sausage, a pudding, a sensitive hound. A curse, a bath, a legacy, an ocean.

■ ■ ■

In a drawing of a family tree in which I am the trunk, underground roots branch below me and splay into infinitesimal hairs, unknown lineage, imperceptible parts of my construction. Were there maniacs among those ancestors? Flagellants? Cannibals? Does their DNA whisper in my veins? And closer to the stem, the kin with names and well-known maladies, are their messages louder in my blood? There were, I know, diabetics, heartless insurance salesmen, a manic-depressive, a convict who died of tooth decay. Will they become me? Will a summons in my blood banish me to the same path as my father, as god-knows-who-else down there in the dark earth with him?

In middle age I still succumb to the bloody rites of fertility, though by now the chances of my having babies has ebbed. This trunk rooted in ten thousand years of genetic material will not bear fruit. Blood, each cell bearing its cargo of DNA, will not make a home for new life. That's all folks, end of the line. Above that trunk are bloodless invisible branches. This is one.

■ ■ ■

Many years ago, I stood on a cliff at Point Lobos and stared at a finger of the Pacific as it nudged the inlet below. The kelp was doing its show of psychedelia, paisleys heaved among the sequins. Sea lions barked and cool air stung my cheeks. My father's ashes had been in the ocean for a few months, his meager ounces mixed with the megatons, more carbon added to the soup. We are different people, I reminded myself. For one thing, I'm alive.

Yet still when I look at my face in the mirror I see my mouth weighed down by his scowl. A shroud of insurmountable failure, his, threatens to swallow me whole. It's a ghost story a frightened child can't shake, even in middle age.

My antidote, that crucifix I hold up to ward off such monsters, is an image of the Pacific, the cliff at Point Lobos, its surf seething below me. And to match that image, I add a little voice-over, recite a childhood rhyme, something I've saved for moments like these, "The world is so full of such wondrous things, I'm sure we should all be as happy as kings." It's too cheery a reflex, I suppose, like whistling in the dark, but it calms my pulse.

Blood drums in my ears. So like the ocean, teeming with its component creatures, red cells, white cells, leukocytes, T's. Cells that nourish, or cells that protect. Some that seal the wounds.

DRUMMER

for Kathy

In a simple drum set—the kind you snuck up to at the dance, the one you tapped furtively while the band was off guzzling punch at the break—there are cymbals, a kick drum and a snare.

The set, if you're right-handed, is laid out in a predictable arrangement. Cymbals are played with the right hand. The ride cymbal delineates the possible beats, pencils in all the corners, *sixty-six, sixty-six, sixty-six*. Each strike is a thin red second hand ticking each stand-and-be-counted moment, a field of brass filaments, a prairie. The crash cymbal serves as punctuation, an exclamation point at the end of a verse—with that *tisssss* we all cheer and catch the wave into the chorus. The *tak-tak-tak* is the snare, domain of the left hand, the verbal mind, the tongue, the mouth. The snare shouts declarations in the foreground, moves us through that prairie like a plow. Lastly, the kick drum *(tum-ta-tum)* is played by the right foot. The kick drum is the rhythm at the root of your being. It throbbed around you when you were only an exploding cell.

In utero, pulsation surrounded us, became us. At four weeks, our hearts took root within the curl of our bodies, and we managed a tintinnabulation of our own. We were both a part of and apart from the amniotic rhythm, a clacker inside a kettledrum.

All mammals breathe once for every four heartbeats. A measure of 4/4 time. We have a natural affinity for fours, our four limbs, the four seasons, the vortices of the compass, the sturdy, if sometimes stodgy, fixedness of a square. Don't forget the four chambers of the heart. Four is our ground, our anchor.

Rhythm expresses the heart's intent, no matter what melodic convolutions the cortex invents.

■ ■ ■

His drums were loud and shiny, commanded a presence like the snaps and pops of a bonfire. He was tall, dark, probably in his thirties, and wore a white sport coat. I was six, traveling with my family in Rome. I sucked spaghetti up through the tiny o of my lips, and marveled at the sheen of his hair. Night after night as my mouth made orange stains on my napkin, his band closed their set with "Arrivederci Roma."

On our last evening in Rome sobs stoppered up my nostrils. How could I bid *arrivederci* to my drummer? My mother consoled me with the drone of a hypnotist. "Tonight you feel your heart will break, but by morning your heart will have turned to stone." Sure enough, like the audience volunteer who wakes from her trance to find her lifelong passion for chocolate snuffed, by morning I was indifferent to the drummer in the white sport coat. My heart had turned to stone.

What was my heart anyway? Why had it thumped wildly inside my chest, and tricked me into thinking I could live the rest of my days in a Roman hotel? How could it choke me with tears at one moment, only to leave me blasé the next?

■ ■ ■

A friend recently saw a sonogram of her father's heart. Through the moonscape lens of sonography, on a small black and white TV, she peered at what looked like a rock in the ocean battered by waves. The crashing of the surf against the rock was, she realized, his heart's convulsion, the beat maintaining his life.

I've imagined the hollows of my heart like the interior of a red pepper, the walls of the chambers stippled and scarlet. The heart's musculature, of course, is less brittle, as taut as the flesh on an endurance swimmer. Atria and ventricles fill up like the locks of Suez. The pockets take turns bloating and squeezing until the blood and its cargo are dispatched back out into the body.

Our everyday image of the heart is the symmetrical bodice, the red satin bustier of valentines, but in reality it's the gory knot at the core of our circulation. A fist-size football, only tougher, it pounds out 100,000 beats a day, 365 days a year, and—knock on wood—eighty years, at least. The heart works like a horse.

■ ■ ■

By junior high I'd jerry-rigged my own method of drumming. I would tap one pencil against my homework. If hit just right, that small stack of binder papers rustled like the soft splash of a cymbal. Meanwhile the pencil in my other hand smacked the ream inside my textbook like the snap of a snare. I copied the riffs, the rolls, the crashes of the R&B songs I heard on my transistor radio.

During the day, the value of x may have occupied my mind, but by the evening, alone with the angst of my adolescence, the energy of R&B was a solace for my heart. Teen magazines worked their hard sell, but as far as I was concerned the hormonal wonderland they professed might as well have been science fiction. Teendom was a setup for failed assimilation. I was bullied into forfeiting the things I did best, to relinquish the feel of used muscles, to say good-bye to a view of the world one can only acquire from the loft of a tree. I despised nylons, girdles, dress shields, the works, and so slinked down the halls of my school with the hunched rebellion of James Dean. I was called a lez.

The music I tuned in to after school became my sanctuary, because within its confines, I could cope with, if not revel in, my solitude. I don't know what invisible force led me to the right end of the AM band, to KDAY, the one R&B station in the Bay Area, rather than to the bubble gum stations on the left end. But once I'd heard the alto voices of the Chiffons chiming "One Fine Day" I was hooked. Theirs was a madrigal beauty that ached a bit, a more interesting flavor than, say, just cream, more like chocolate which, because of its bittersweetness, won me, hands down. Then there was Smokey Robinson and the Miracles' "Shop Around," the Orlons' "Don't Hang Up," the Drifters' "Up on the Roof." I couldn't wait to return to my room so that I could isolate myself with the freshness of those rhythms, the glory of those harmonies, and the often hilarious stories of characters like Nadine and Johnny B. Goode. I was diving headfirst into insularity, but I was also learning about a larger world where the rules of gender were differently drawn.

No less masculine, only more intense, Smokey's voice soared in falsetto, so too, little Anthony's, Eddie Hendricks'. Dinah Washington's voice cut, abraded, teased. Her expression was large, not diminutive. Inside its breadth I recognized the timbre of authority, a summons to discover my own expression. I wasn't suited to the indignities of cinched waists, padded bras, gouging garters. Listening to Dinah's sass, Aretha's fire or Martha Reeves's brawn I was closer to being my own creature, a tiger burning in the night.

Remember the roll that begins "Dancing in the Street"?

Calling for a revolution of global proportions, to let the spirit of celebration overtake the habit of repression. *Calling out around the world, are you ready for a brand new beat?* Under this anthem's spell we would disobey the laws of curfew or traffic. *Summer's here, and the time is right for dancin' in the street.* We would have no fear of crime or of the police. A call to arms of the Emma Goldman variety, the celebrative side of the civil rights movement, *All we need is music, sweet sweet music.*

■ ■ ■

Music is most certainly compulsion, the repetition that most assuredly will set things right. Percussion, then, is the architecture of compulsion. The temple in which instruments daven, genuflect, cadenza. The drummer is the vertebrae for a body of tonalities.

Drumming is a distillation not only of time, but of that organizing principle we call math. One may bring the language of mathematics to rhythm, translate double time into a series of fractions. Corral the zealous, tapping feet into a set of quarter notes. But one needn't be fluent in math to have a profound understanding of these thumps, tics and snaps. One can play by ear, by heart, by savancy. Percussion can play itself directly through the body without having to go through a scribe in the mind.

A drummer's genius is not narrative. The tonalities produced by drums do not approximate the human voice, or the cries of animals. There is no subject, no protagonist, no hero's journey. Whatever virtuosity a drummer might display, it's ultimately an embellishment on the rhythmic territory. On one level, a drummer's sensibility is like a mason's sensibility. Each brick is laid tight into the grid, a sure and solid thing. Today follows yesterday, as will tomorrow, today. In laying the bricks for this temple, drumming is an attempt to improve on that primeval chamber where Absolute Grace was comprehended in 4/4.

Sometimes the percussive genius veers off in defiance of the grid—a gap appears in the wall—a syncopation, a window. Our bodies respond to it. We ache for the safe enclosures of repetition, and are spellbound by a view. Syncopation withholds the teat, expectation is teased. The missing heartbeat resounds within the inner ear, tethers us to the hungers in our blood. The pulse is always amniotic, we remember the fish we were, we curl and thrust for immersion, just as exquisitely as we breach for an unknown.

■ ■ ■

In 1961 I met Kathy at summer camp. I don't know what invisible force led me to her, has led me, time and time again, to a sympathetic soul. She was an oddly joyous child, whose zeal and whose lack of WASPy virtues made her unpopular at an early age. Like me, she was an outsider. Too effusive, motherless since early childhood, she had orange kinky hair that spread itself out in every direction as though suspended, like sargassum, in water. The kids at her school taunted her and called her "steel wool."

Where someone else might have dumped me for not knowing the ropes at camp, Kathy hung out with me. Though she was already an accomplished trail rider, she accompanied me to the remedial corral, where the horse illiterate got their first taste of the saddle, and where a palomino pony lived his last senile days in a clockwise circle.

Astride Welsh Boy, the walk was a piece of cake. Getting to a canter was the hard part, not only because Welsh Boy had long since lost his joie de vivre, but because the intermediary gait, the trot, was impossibly bouncy, and usually ended with my being sprung from his back. While I waited on the sidelines for my next shot at equestrian glory, Kathy would sit with me and critique my style. "Grip with your knees," she'd advise, or "lean forward." "Try and relax your hips."

One day I forgot my rookie self-consciousness. I wanted nothing more than for Welsh Boy to canter and let him know my resolve. My body spoke an unmistakable idiom. We loped around the corral like Roy and Trigger, like The Lone Ranger and Silver, like Ginger and Fred, his back rocking me as smoothly as a hobbyhorse.

Kathy had given me the confidence to ride. I was no longer a nerd. I had, in fact, discovered a haven in this summer camp, a respite from the rigors of what I considered to be inane femininity. Throughout junior high we continued our summer camp alliance, sought refuge in that tomboy oasis, until we were finally reunited year-long in the same boarding school.

The Athenian School, like many progressive liberal arts schools of the sixties, was a safe haven for creeps like Kathy and me, rejects of the prep school industry. Both of us felt we could discover ourselves there without reproach. At weekend dances, Kathy pranced and spun with her whole heart, wailed, off-key, along with Otis Redding's "Try a Little Tenderness." Everyone loved to dance with her or at least near her. She gave herself to each song, moved with her elbows, shoulders and knees, like a hillbilly, like a chicken. Kathy blossomed, more popular than any prom queen might have been, had there been any.

I too left my old skin behind, and even my anal penmanship relaxed into a scrawl that is wholly my own. My old misery persisted only through the word *lez*. *Lez* lodged inside me like a burr. It had come to name me, to claim the longing I was supposed to outgrow. After classes I'd often seek out Kathy for solace, for her no-nonsense counsel. In the afternoon, orange light and neroli incense suffused her room, and the turntable whispered a scratchy version of Donovan's "Wear Your Love

Like Heaven." "Lowe," she'd say, "whatever's in your heart is good." At the end of my senior year she wrote in my yearbook, "I wish I could stop you from worrying about being a lesbian. Since Henry D. Thoreau uses better words than me, here is a quote: *If a man does not keep pace with his companions, perhaps it is because he hears a different drummer. Let him step to the music which he hears, however measured or far away.* Have confidence in yourself because I do."

She had long since dismissed the values of assimilation that had been turned viciously upon her in childhood. Already on her own course, she embraced the realm of anomaly. Hers was a crackpot drum that marched her toward an adult life out of earshot of conventions. Even in her thirties, Kathy never straightened her hair. Her leg hair, too, remained staunchly natural, unshaven—a gutsy stand for a straight woman in posthippie, postfeminist times. Kathy, or Kit as she renamed herself, lived for two things: the children she worked with in her profession as a physical therapist, and kayaking. It's easy to picture her beaming from her kayak like a tomboy on a trail ride, rolling with the bucking water, her hair natural, kinky, on fire.

■ ■ ■

Many years after high school I stood on a balcony at the Circus Disco in Hollywood and surveyed a roomful of men moving in unison to "The Hustle." I realized, looking over that army of lovers, that my coming out was part of a larger social revolution.

Ours was a culture that felt a strong identification with other ethnic outsiders. Homos danced the pagan rhythms, spoke the outlaw's idiom. The mainstream feared our sexuality, so we got down and celebrated it. Disco was our call to arms. *Do a little dance. Make a little love. Get Down Tonight!*

Characterized by the open high hat on the strike before the

down beat, a layering of rhythmic patterns, and a thundering bass beat, disco flaunted a Latin flavor, a pagan spice. It was a force to be reckoned with from the waist down. Like all African-derived music, disco—despite its co-option by Donny and Marie—was dance music, community music, an anthem for liberation.

■ ■ ■

I finally got to play the drums. I did, at last, hear the proper pop of a snare rather than the dull thud my history textbook once offered. The rustle of papers finally was realized as the sizzle of big brass cymbal.

I played in The Love Machine. Like any garage band we practiced weekly surrounded by old cans of paint and motor oil, the walls and ceiling sound-proofed by a few hundred egg cartons. I wasn't *terrible*, not as steady as Ringo, but better by far than Dennis Wilson. My biggest handicap was a sluggish left hand, and so I practiced the paradiddle, the drummer's dogged rosary, an exercise that promotes ambidexterity.

Like many garage bands we celebrated the sophomoric, but unlike most, we were all-girl, and lezzy at that. Our vulgarity had, we liked to think, a uniquely low-brow edge to it. We altered the lyrics of oldies to suit our "womyn loving womyn" sensibilities. "Woolly Bully," the sixties TexMex hit became "Fluffy Muffy." The rocker "Born on the Bayou" transformed into "Born in a Test Tube," a paean for artificial insemination.

Though part of our shtick was irreverence, I was never without awe for the bright sounds produced from my drum set, sounds that riveted me to the present. I've never since experienced anything as joyful as playing with that group, being the backbone, supplying the beat. I'm only sorry Kit didn't see me play. I'm sure she would have cheered me on. As if, still sitting outside the corral, she'd urge me to go another round until I got it right.

■ ■ ■

Look, it's an autumn afternoon and the clear light has gone golden and the leaves on the trees as far as you can see in every direction are ablaze. But stretching even beyond what can be seen, is their collective bluster, like the seething of a gargantuan sea. These are the cymbal's strokes. And each tree your horse passes adds to the immensity.

The snare is the bronc carrying you through this landscape. You can't help but time your exhalation to his pace, can't keep your breath from falling with his hooves on the dust. Wherever your thoughts may take you this afternoon, you can't entirely leave his motion. His muscles roll beneath you, and his gait measures a rhythm that becomes, for the both of you, a joy.

And here with your heart beating fiercely with the knowledge of being alive at that moment is the steady kick drum. You, dear rider, are borne into this golden afternoon, as you were into the resounding sac of your mother's belly.

■ ■ ■

Kit died. Her kayak overturned and her head struck a rock. She was found in the bend of a river, an inverted Medusa, her hair like coils of magma cooling under water.

It's said that when a person has drowned the heart endures even after the brain's been strangled. What rhythms do hearts invent, what slow but ardent tempos can they keep, when no one's left to hear them?

And if, as some after-death experiences attest, the brain persists a while after the last heartbeat, what shape would our final thoughts take as they drift through our silent bodies, for the first time without accompaniment of a drum?

■

It's taken me several decades, but I've learned to listen to my heart. By this I mean I've learned to listen both to the emotional organ—the timpani who marched me toward a bed where a woman lies waiting, the drummer Kit advised me to follow—and to the biological heart, the gory pump, who toils ever faithfully on my behalf. At night when the anxious chatter of my thoughts makes Nod an impossible destination, I've learned to focus on the stalwart metronome inside me. My heart's spasms feel like a soft pat on my back, the body's show of support. I relax.

And as I pay more attention to my heart, it gradually evades me. The sly organ slows when I hush to it. It insists it is merely an accompanist, not a soloist. The quieter I become, the more it softens, until its seesaw is a lullaby.

In those few still moments when I'm alone with my own modest rhythm, before dreams waltz away with my attention, I'm filled with a love simply for being alive, for the invisible force that squeezes my ventricles, that locks and unlocks the rubine chambers, time after time, with a comforting, palpable *thump*.

MOTHERS AND OTHERS, BUT ALSO BROTHERS

For most of my early childhood my mother and I had a bedtime ritual. She would sit on the edge of my bed rubbing my back. Then she'd lean forward and kiss my ear. The warmth of my mother's breath seeped into my brain like a balm, and consummated the day with a whispered ". . . there now." I wanted nothing more than that, the satisfaction of her words breathed into me. To be reassured, however falsely, lips pressed to ear, that no harm would come.

And if I stayed up beyond my mother's bedtime, as I did when I grew older, my father came in and kissed my mouth. It was an open-mouthed kiss that made me all too familiar with the insides of his cheeks and left my mouth clotted with bourbon. Every night alcohol paraded through his blood like bad religion. Some nights the bourbon's zeal erupted into riots, windows were smashed, cupboards kicked in. Mornings I found rooms in ruin.

But I was not without stalwart male role models. I had three older brothers. They were trees in whose shade I grew strong. I grew like a tree, too, with possibilities branching unabashedly in every direction.

Richard was closest in age, only six years older. His pale skin, like mine, was flecked with brown, and his breath smelled like root beer. Richard taught me not only to dig forts, to fish, and to whittle but to use my imagination in games, to create characters. I played "Speedy" to Richard's "Skyhawk." Gorgeous George, the good wrestler, to his villain, The Sheik. We made tommy guns out of blocks of wood spray painted silver. And when we snaked through ivy, we ensnared Nazis in ambush, liberated French villages.

Stephen told me stories and showed me, as though teaching me to mold with clay, how to write my first words: *act,* then *fact,* and from there, *factory.* His shoes were large enough to fit the length of my lower arms, so I crawled around his bedroom in them, like a seal pup. Stephen paid me a nickel for half-hour back rubs. And when I lifted up his shirt, and touched the enormity of his back, his skin smelled like sleep, a rich broth of cream and potatoes.

Peter smelled the most like wood, a piece of oak split open, a pile of raked leaves. Peter waxed philosophical with me, often bedazzling my imagination. Sharing his belief, for example, that the universe was female and nature surely male. And once, while we were watching a ewe in labor, he theorized that the pain of childbirth was mollified by a sense of expectation, making it "a good pain."

All three teased me, handled me, but never harmed me. With my brothers, trespassing boundaries was never an issue. Brothers were Lancelots, guardians, fellow travelers. They enjoyed my tomboyness. They were, in fact, agents of it. So, partially out of gratitude and partially out of awe, I fell in love with each of them.

■ ■ ■

I remember the exact moment I stopped playing, the exact moment when childhood snapped shut: I was twelve, sitting on a hill, looking down through a grove of buckeye trees with Dorothy, a playmate three years younger. She was pleading with me to choose from our assortment of fantasy games. The ground was littered with fallen buckeyes. I turned one over in my hands. The seed was moist, heavy, cleaved into globes like a dog's testicles.

"Spies?" she begged. "Tramps? Indian scouts?"

"I'm too old to play," I announced, trying on maturity like a hand-me-down.

Up until that moment, I had prided myself on being a tomboy. Tomboy meant that, among playmates, I was Alpha, aviator of the game's plot. Like my brothers before me, I could rev the game or land it, veer it in any direction, urge, as a film director might, deeper role-playing, a more satisfying scene. Tomboy meant I trusted the structure of tree limbs. Meant I knew the physics of flat stones against a taut skin of water. Meant I could slither into a hole in the dirt, a hollow in the brush. Meant I simply had to put my body into, onto, and through things.

But looking down that hill, I struggled with a new definition. Tomboy meant something sinister, what schoolmates in the city were beginning to call me, lez, Miss L, Miss H. Queer.

■ ■ ■

A convert to midcentury child psychology, my mother embraced the term arrested development as an explanation of deviance, and also as a substitute, albeit a more sophisticated one, for bad.

When my devotions toward female teachers persisted into high school, my mother preached her belief that those crushes constituted a mere phase. Adults who never grew out of that stage could expect the same distant pity as persons suffering from dwarfism or mental retardation. I would grow out of that phase, she assured me, though her ministrations had the ring of commandments. I wanted to believe I would. I too began to perceive homosexuality as an emotional defect, damaged goods. Something inferior to the robust pageantry of normal longing.

At the same time I studied my mother's attractions for clues to the correct form of desire. During summers, the afternoon sun chased us behind the veil of venetian blinds, into the gloom of our house, to watch Merv and his guests. Within the cool light of daytime TV I could turn my face to hers and examine her reactions. My mother's eyes danced to (irony of ironies) the antics of Peter Allen, the suave musings of Vincent Price, the absurd quips of Paul Lynde. She loved these men, plain as day.

I suspect that I mimicked my mother's tastes until they were my own. Soon I too could zero in on that unmistakable something. I thought Laurence Olivier and Rock Hudson were men with enormous sex appeal and, now I realize, not without that certain je ne sais quoi. Was I unknowingly drawn to gay men because of the model of my mother? Or because, as a budding Miss H, I was protected by them from the failure of heterosexual contact?

Because gay men reminded me more of brothers than of fathers?

Until I came out, I might as well have been a gay man, for male was the only gender I could spot in the "pathology" of same-sex love. In the sixties, as far as I knew, there were no novels with lesbian protagonists, no *Sappho Was a Right-on Woman*, no *Lesbian Nation*. Instead, I read *Giovanni's Room*, saw *Boys in the Band*. I eyed my mother's string of interior decorators. I listened for clues to my own stirrings in the swells and swirls of Tchaikovsky's music.

At sixteen, I was consumed by his *Pathétique*. It was the first piece of music (non-Beatle, nonjazz) that I listened to as closely as I would a friend. Before this I had never been able to perceive the structure of a complex composition.

The symphony's form is as legible as a graph of the Dow on

a bad day. Scales try to ascend, but succumb finally to decline. For a glowing moment it is Sisyphus nearing the top, before gravity bullies it back. The symphony is built like a mania trying to wriggle out of despair, like a life struggling to free itself from the inevitability of death. Like (or so the legend goes) the composer finally crushed by his own unspeakable perversion.

Did our music instructor suggest this was homosexuality's anthem? Or did I only imagine he did? I was continually on guard. It seemed everywhere I went, everything I read whispered about homosexuality, with the hiss of impending disaster. Lisping boys carried their loneliness through the American South, past ads for Nehi sodas, into dark, mysterious thickets. Some left home for dingy rooms in sea towns, to sleep with sailors who invariably dumped them. Some, like Capote, grew degenerate, whining incoherently on late-night talk shows. The homosexuality of men, while literate, seemed doomed to cataclysm.

■ ■ ■

I like to say the earth shook the day I met him. February 11, 1971, the day of the Sylmar quake. I had moved to L.A. to go to art school, but I'd long stopped showing up for classes. I was spending my nights alone, watching TV in an apartment I shared with a woman I secretly wanted. I assumed I would spend the rest of my life like that, shrinking within a self-imposed quarantine.

That morning jolted me into quite a different world. My bed pitched like a runaway stagecoach. The old Frigidaire lurched like Frankenstein into the center of the kitchen. When I pulled on my clothes and fled the building, I knew that nothing about my life would be the same. I drove toward the dorm, toward new friends, toward rescue. The sun set brighter that night, and I remember the moon had an orange sheen, maybe from the dust the temblor had stirred up.

We spent all of our time together after I moved into the dorm. I was first struck by his voice—earthy and masculine, but buoyant, playful, almost musical. He looked completely different from any man my age. He had short hair, a rabbinical beard, and wire-rim glasses. He wore baggy wool trousers. One leg had a plastic patch of a puppy ironed on the knee. And when he sat cross-legged on my bed and listened to my gospel records with his eyes closed, I could stare shamelessly at the length and curl of his eyelashes.

Bernard had a way of looking at things. He turned me on to pop art, to the stunning beauty of ordinary, mass-produced objects. The grocery store was a latent museum, and all the shoppers collectors. The exalted realm of Art was democratized, the simple objects of the world were ripe for the picking.

One day, in the spirit of pop, we created a meal out of Play-Doh. White for the blubbery stripe that banked the chop. Yellow for the slab that sagged like an Oldenburg on a mound of peas. Each pea was a small wad of green, rolled into a perfect bead. And as we rolled and molded the clay with childlike abandon, our words falling easily between us, I could smell Bernard, or what I thought was Bernard, all the elements of a brother's scent: clay and salt, root beer and wood, cream and mashed potatoes.

I don't remember who ventured "I think I might be a homosexual" first. But regardless, our bond was sealed that day by those words. And for the first time, because we mirrored the same secret, we each stole a new glimpse of ourselves, each strutted a bit in the other's reflection, a cockiness that our hidden oddity might in fact make us "special." We developed a style of humor that lampooned the burlesque extremes of heterosexuality. Gender seemed an absurdity, and we had no scruples about mocking all its Mamie Van Dorens and Victor Matures. Years later I would recognize our joking as camp, the gay currency, the stuff upon which a worldview is crafted. I would also see, with the enhancement of hindsight, that the intimacy we were building would forge a lifetime partnership.

We found a house to rent in the northeast corner of the Valley. Twenty years ago Sylmar was a hodgepodge community of students, bikers, and young families, tenants who enjoyed cheap rents after owners fled the quake's epicenter. At night, even months after the quake, dogs resumed pack behavior and could be seen trotting down darkened boulevards. Poodles, bulldogs, hounds, Chihuahuas, all ganged together, drawn by the undertow catastrophe sets in motion. Tumbleweeds roamed too on nights when the Santa Anas blew. The whole world, in fact, had a feral snarl to it. Only eighteen months before, the decade of flower power had fallen into dissolution when Manson's cult massacred Sharon Tate and her friends in a Southland canyon. Marvin Gaye sang "Mercy, Mercy Me" and "What's Goin' On?" Up the freeway a mile or so, the rubble from a toppled overpass lay in ruin like a fallen civilization.

Mind you, all the upheaval was second nature to us. We were veterans of upheaval. Both had been bruised by a father's tantrums. Bernard's adolescence was shaken—not once but twice—by the loss of brothers to cancer. I had witnessed my father's sodden decline into suicide. And both understood how our secret desires, once exposed, would only provoke further havoc and loss. The notion of living on a fault line seemed to us as ordinary as, say, pretending to be straight.

Did I mention Bernard and I were living together with another couple? They were a real couple, while we were still chaste, just good friends. Night after night they murmured behind their bedroom wall while we sat up in the living room listening to records. Their bodies seemed virile, sinewy; while mine, in its unrelenting virginity, had become as insubstantial as light on a movie screen. And Bernard's flesh, what was that to me? An amalgam of shadows?

One night Bernard and I both confessed that we had each recently masturbated. He said, "God, it's so ridiculous. We should have had sex with each other!" And so we decided, there and then, that, yes, in fact, we'd better. Moments later we each bathed in anticipation of the great deflowering. During his shower, Bernard had doused his body hair with cream rinse. During mine, forget that I had masturbated the night before, my body was entirely new. The touch of my own soapy hand was different, as it slid lather along a female body just beginning to take form, just beginning to gather density and heat.

We emerged from the solitude of those showers, like Quakers from a silent prayer, grateful for the ease of each other's friendship, eager to taste what lay ahead: three nights rolling in the amber glow of a space heater, the obsolescence of my twin bed, the deepening of our intimacy.

And why not? I trusted Bernard more than anyone I knew. We were best friends, and we were attracted to each other. It was perfect. Except for one thing. The "shared secret" of our homosexuality, the disclosure that initially welded us together, suddenly loomed like a lunatic who had to be carefully subdued.

Nevertheless, no matter how we struggled to suppress it, once we had started living as lovers Bernard's interest in men only got stronger. Our first summer was a nightmare of tanned pectorals, deltoids, and quadriceps. The seasonal display of masculine flesh confounded Bernard, and threatened to undermine our future. Of course, I was continually aroused by women, but felt more acutely the need to hold on to my first relationship as though it were my last. I could keep arousal safely shelved, could even ignore the portents of our breakup, because, quite simply, we were in love. As I watched him suffer his attractions to men I panicked and urged him to seek therapy. He went, half-hoping he might change, half-trying to keep what was good about us from shattering, like a fragile dowry, into a billion unrecognizable bits.

We stayed together three years, during which time we did everything a real couple does—laughed, worked, argued, had sex, went on diets. The pain of breaking apart was dampened by the inevitable exploration of same-sex love, pain my brother Peter might have reasoned "good."

It's a rare day Bernard and I don't speak to each other on the phone at least once. He, too, is my brother; more so, my twin, though my hair has gone white while his recedes. We still laugh, argue, and diet together. We've grown in tandem as writers, sharing our discovery of favorite poems, helping each other to shape our works. The only thing we don't do is fondle each other, or share the kind of open-heartedness fondling encourages. In many ways we are still a couple, a couple for whom a sexual impasse has meant anything but estrangement.

In the days when my lesbianism steeped me in a separatist community, Bernard would joke about being worried he'd inadvertently leave hairs in my house—evidence I'd been visited by a masculine presence. Needless to say, some of my girlfriends have been threatened by my commitment to Bernard, a man, the hirsute embodiment of Patriarchy. Or more importantly by my commitment to a relationship that continues to nourish our hearts and minds, that once was sexual, but worse, that is steadfastly lifelong.

■ ■ ■

How can I explain to my mother that despite all her pleading with me to grow beyond my homosexuality, I've remained intractable, true to myself? Shall I confirm her suspicions that, yes, her behaviors may have caused my own? That a woman's kisses pressed to my ear still reassure me beyond words? Or rather, that I am, simply, like Popeye, what I am. Can I admit, without her thrilling to false hopes, that, having loved a man, having mated with a man, I know I could still?

I still find men attractive, and I still recall, with sexual excitement, my escapades into heterosexual sex. I especially enjoyed the encyclopedic range of sexual imagery to draw from, the gamut, from Bible to porno, an endless array. Not to mention the hundred cinematic kisses that left me breathless in the dark. Like Kim Novak and William Holden dancing to "Moonglow" in a July swelter.

Yet when a woman approaches I feel something older, less articulate. Something as absolutely hoped for as "there now." This is my polemic, justification for my nature. We all inevitably feel the pull toward some creature made luminous in the act of love. Is it toward the archetypal Momma? Or the, if you're so inclined, Daddy? If all the world's faiths can sing the virtues of the Great Mother and Father, can these sex-inspired hallucinations be so pathological? Aren't all humans linked together by a need that predates adult development, when surrender was the mirror image of survival? When, at our most vulnerable, we were literally lifted up into the air toward the salvation of an adult body? Likewise, aren't our sucking lovers briefly infants? Their need for us is as primal as milk. Is it childish to employ our imaginations in the service of our pleasures? Is our development arrested, or are our natures finally realized?

Besides, look again: what once seemed *Pathétique* is now sleek and predacious, like a spy snaking through ivy, a scout probing a new stand of trees. Like you surrounded by buckeyes as childhood snaps open. You, stepping over fallen columns, liberating French villages. While dogs howl beyond the woods, you undress and slip into the bath. The lather rolling in your hands makes its sucking sound. You will always find fascination in the flesh around the nipple, the back of the neck. As Bernard will when Brian comes home tonight. Not for the sake of procreation, not for some higher purpose or polemic. Bernard, you, me, us all, our fingers branching, unabashed.

MARTIAN SIGHTING IN HOLLYWOOD

1974, my last year of art school, my last year with Bernard. The same year the cops woke us at five, the helicopter hovering over our cottage and a bullhorn booming above the rattle, "Lock your doors, don't go outside! There is a wounded suspect in your area . . . he is armed and dangerous!" And Bernard and I in that instant, our eyes locking across the pillow, envisioned the identical image of Charles Manson hiding in the backseat of our VW. The very same year we rented our cottage in Hollywood from an ex-hippie musician, who was "a close personal friend" of Mick Jagger, and who only the year before rented our cottage to Linda Ronstadt. It was in this house that we listened to bootlegged tapes from KPFK of Patty Hearst's denunciation of her bourgeois upbringing. Patty had lived next door to my friend Nancy in Berkeley the night she was abducted by the Symbionese Liberation Army. Still, we were sure it was all a big media event, a happening brought to you by the CIA, because the national obsession was still Watergate and the administration was hungry to distract the public with smarmy conspiracy stories involving white heiresses and black revolutionaries with Afros. This was the same year a black wino wandered into our groovy cottage, looked at us, hallucinated Tanya Hearst and Bill Harris, and asked to use our telephone to turn us over to the authorities. The same year Stevie Wonder sang "Livin' Just Enough for the City." The same year Cinque and his cohorts fried before our eyes in a televised shoot-out live from Compton. The year Cambodia was bombed.

That was the year I took to hiding my dope in the vacuum cleaner. The year my friend Cris showed up at our doorstep in her black leather jacket after hitching and screwing her way across the country. The year Bernard's friend Sarah became a student of the Dalai Lama after traveling to Nepal, the year I started eating brown rice, the year Nixon resigned.

In 1974, two lesbian friends came to live with us for a month before driving to Guatemala. We moved our TV out of the bedroom and into the living room so the four of us could smoke dope and watch TV and work ourselves into an apocalyptic frenzy. Between news, talk shows, and science fiction B movies, the world took on the semblance of a kitsch police state—a radioactive world patrolled by Godzillas, Mothras and Rodans.

We took color slides of one another sleeping or eating, but mostly clicked away at the TV as though we were pilfering shards from an alien culture. The four of us made a happy-enough family, despite our collective paranoia and the momentum we were gaining smoking pot.

One night, two guys came on "The Dick Cavett Show" and told their story of being taken onboard a flying saucer. Apparently they were fishing in the Mississippi when they saw the ball of blue light. Oh, sure they admitted they had downed a couple of Buds, but what they saw that night was no pink elephant. The extraterrestrials had sucked them up into their saucer through some kind of luminous straw. Then they frisked the geezers with a mechanical eye. It must have been a hypnotic one at that, because the next thing these guys knew they were stark naked and back on the river. No wallets, no shoes, no fish.

At one point the ever-wry Cavett held up an artist's rendering of the aliens based on the guys' descriptions. It had that dead-pan quality of police composites, except all the elements were strictly slapstick—octopus arms, lobster claws, Big Bird torso, bat ears and an empty place where a mouth should have been—all tossed together and tidily rendered, all very straightforward and serious, as if the logical next step involved a dragnet in outer space.

But despite the absurdity of that image, however much it looked like an episodic drawing passed among surrealists, or some hokey celluloid spook complete with zippers, the look on the faces of the two guys from Mississippi was chilling. That reminder sent them into a state of shock. It was the kind of panic that rang true, not the simpering wide-eyed theatrics of a Chester or even a Dr. McCoy. This was the real thing, unabashed terror on a talk show. Something altogether too intimate.

How can I describe how all this was beginning to affect me? All these many months of travelers, with their alien sexual ways, their probing eyes? All the many races battling one another while Rome crumbles in a blaze? The line between art and life was being rubbed out—and only the pink flecks of an eraser lay scattered like ashes around me. Someone I feared, was doing it to me. Someone, more strange than I could even imagine, was seeping into my mind, like cyanide under a door.

A few weeks later, our lesbian friends packed up their van. They put a red bandanna around the neck of their German shepherd, slapped their thighs to urge her to come. And once she had settled into the back, "Moon Cat" was carried onboard, held on the lap of the one riding shotgun. Bernard and I stood at the end of the drive. We waved them a fond "Aloha" as their bus faded off into the tan haze at the end of Highland Avenue.

That night the strangest thing happened. I found myself sitting upright in bed at midnight, the clock brimming with phosphorescent digits, projecting a pale green glaze on Bernard's body. I felt I had woken into the core chamber of an emerald, every surface seemed gem-bright, lucid, fixed in the moment. I had the uncanny sensation of being suspended somewhere between dread and anticipation, an anxiety one sometimes experiences in dreams.

At any rate, I became very aware of the sound of breath, my own and then Bernard's. I listened to the way in which our breathing became syncopated. I watched his chartreuse chest rise and fall. I heard the sound of our breathing in unison, and then the other sound—not quite like breathing—the other sound that slowly drew itself into me, the sound fear makes. My ear then was an enormous gaping window with all the curtains flapping. The emerald had shattered and what followed was a silence like the one after a glass is broken in public.

And then, it was as if a giant cookie cutter was pressing itself into the door of my closet, an outline of a figure was being welded by someone on the other side, until finally there stood a schematic cutout of a being, something like those symbols you see on the doors of rest rooms, but completely luminous, blindingly luminous in fact. Light in the form of a gingerbread figure. Someone without features, fingers or genitals, just radiance the color of magma. And around the blaze of its body was some kind of sparking ectoplasm, tiny whips of lightning that snaked and cracked and spun lights around the walls of the room like a disco ball.

We gaped at each other for several minutes. I must have seemed dull and lifeless, as imploded and dense as a dark star. Perhaps it thought we humans feed on the green energy of clocks, or that we worship time with them. In any case, it must have sensed the fleeting nature of my proteins, the unstable wisdom of my DNA, and found me as primitive as a trilobite.

Perhaps this was the sort of being people saw when they saw angels, visitors who come in the night and leave their hosts quaking like helpless children. Guests whose farewell finds us alone in the dark, staring up at the heavens.

So what, you may well ask, does all this mean? No words of wisdom were imparted, no messiahs were conceived. Was it all a dream? Had the membrane between art and life been punctured? Had I reached my threshold of pot and TV? Did it mean that Bernard and I were to become estranged? That I was to become a lesbian myself and live with a cat? That Patty Hearst would become a case study among hostages, that *terrorism* was to become a household word? That "Star Trek" would become ever more popular, that Linda Ronstadt would live in the governor's mansion, that an actor would become president, that Watergate would transfigure into this-gate and that-gate, future episodes of a bad docudrama?

Helicopters continue their nightly vigil over Hollywood, their beams probing the avenues. The streets are always being reassembled and I can barely recognize them. I continue to read the face of my clock, and my mirror grows more alien each year, a parody of the blaze inside me.

ESSENTIAL BODIES

It's a mass on the left ovary," the doctor says, "... roughly the size of a grapefruit." If it's not an abscess, this doctor continues, he'll take it out, maybe tomorrow. If it's not an abscess, and it's the size of a grapefruit, what kind of monstrosity is it?

Six hours after we rush into Emergency, Susan's wheeled up to a hospital bed. The good news is that the Demerol has finally dulled her pain. Is it cancer? Is Susan in danger? Everything's too fast to know how I feel. I stroke her hand. I go home, feed her cats. I climb into our bed, try to sleep.

Like a child, I try to bargain with the universe for her well-being. Part of me still believes in magic. Part of me still hankers for the theater of the torch-lit cave, the special chant, the right mask, the exact ceremonial step. I think of things I can sacrifice for her, my personal Isaacs: home, health, arms, legs. I make stupid vows like I'll never drink coffee again, or no more masturbation. I try not to think of the big C, as though a thought could trigger the devil's handiwork, and cause Susan's DNA to corkscrew into oblivion.

The mass is already there, it's either cancer or it isn't. There are no spells I can weave, no bargains I can wager that will influence the outcome of the pathologist's report.

I try to reconcile myself to this cold-blooded fact, the indifference with which Chaos cuts the deck. How can my will mean so little?

I imagine Susan in her hospital room, far from the oasis of this bed where our hands find each other in sleep. Is she awake too? That room is dim, open to the bright hallway. Visitors are long gone. Mrs. Brown snores on the other side of the curtain.

The IV drips antibiotic into Susan's forearm. Is she as afraid as I am of the dark under her bed?

■ ■ ■

Most of the day of Susan's surgery I funnel my anxiety into a mistrust of the OB-GYN. He's frosty and officious, barely acknowledges my presence. He might have a bad case of doctoritis, or (another worry to add to my growing list) he may be incurably homophobic. He may venerate procreation and the heterosexual union, view a life's unfolding as a mere prelude to reproduction.

Surely, even in his line of work, he must see a fair number of dykes. Besides, how could anyone whose hands manipulate gore hold any illusions about life's purpose?

The bad news is that, despite all my wishes, despite my petitions to the heavens, the mass is malignant.

The good news is that, despite my doubts in him, and with no help from my magic, the doctor is able to remove the cancer from Susan's body.

In no time Susan's incision transforms into Susan's scar, a tough thin ribbon of flesh, as slick as Ziploc. Skin is a language we all understand, a mannered, sociable suit, a medium for display. It bristles and blushes. It softens to the touch. Susan is restored to the world of emotions, light-years from blood and odd cells.

■ ■ ■

Two weeks later I'm in New Mexico with my friend Nan. She's a New York sculptor on a speaking engagement at the university. For thirteen years our relationship has survived the distance between our cities, nurtured by conversations on the phone. Now we're traveling together in this land of religious art, of wooden Catholic retables where blood drips from stigmata like sap, where even the food is drenched in red, the blood-broth of chilis.

At the university, Nan talks candidly about her battles with cancer. She shows slides of some of her older work. The projector flashes up images of clay torsos, each without a breast. She says she made these pieces to save her own life, to purge herself of terror and conflict. Yet for me there's more here than her particular healing process. These neoclassic figures, rendered as though they were museum remnants—headless, limbless—are the Winged Victories, the Venus de Milos of our era. Breastless Venus is all the more "classically beautiful" for her loss.

These days Nan is making altars in which breasts or penises are nailed to crosses, laid to rest in coffins, wrapped gently in shrouds. In her work, the human body, so forsaken by Christian dogma, is elevated to godhead. Within these altars, flesh, particularly sexual flesh, is no longer profane, but in possession of Christ's attributes: both oppressed and invincible, agonized and forgiving. In this time when AIDS and breast cancer are pandemic, these elegiac icons reaffirm the humanity of sex.

That night after the lecture Nan and I drive into the countryside above Santa Fe to soak in the baths of Ojo Caliente. As soon as our headlights catch the sign for the turnoff, I see we have driven into a time warp. Hippies, old ones, glide with perfect spinal alignment on the paths between buildings. The sixties, in all its sweetness and lack of cynicism, still thrives among these cryogenic adobes, replete with granny glasses and Indian print dresses. I can't stop poking fun at the place; but deep down inside I'm nervous. I'm afraid of seeing Nan's naked body. It's like being afraid to consider the big C, afraid the sight of scars will tunnel me back toward the dark under Susan's bed.

We both choose the individual arsenic baths over the communal iron-water pool. The towels we're given carry the smoke of piñon incense and patchouli oil. We hear a tape of New Age music, birdsong mixed over a droning piano.

As we approach the baths, I feel we have entered a grotto. I smell mildew and hear the echoes of distant drips. We are directed into private rooms, each with a tub. The piano still drones, now over the songs of ocean mammals. The bath tastes both viscous and metallic, like blood. Under its surface my limbs look distended and blue. This is the first rest since the roller coaster began weeks ago in Emergency, but I feel as if I'm still sinking. I feel I'm suffocating inside the *idea* of the body, drowning inside my own viscera.

Later we dress, slowed by our loosened muscles, and I finally see Nan's scar. I'm surprised to find that, after all my apprehension, I'm not frightened by what I see. She is (how idiotic of me not to have guessed) exactly like the subject of all her artwork, the invincible one-breasted Venus I've known and loved all these years. She is still the friend whose disembodied, melodious voice travels to me via telephone.

And I realize that, should Susan get sick again, I won't care if she's disfigured by further surgery. Though I love all the slopes and hillocks of her body, it's not the body alone that moves me. It's how she inhabits it, how she spirits it.

■ ■ ■

I always pictured my anatomy like the bodies illustrated in science textbooks, all the organs in cartographers' pastel shades.

Nerves were etched across these landscapes like aqueducts. The branching arteries were red as interstates, the veins blue highways. In some books, anatomical systems were printed on leaves of acetate so that they could be layered, each upon each, like the ingredients in a submarine sandwich.

Then there was the Visible Woman. Within her see-through flesh, colorful organs conformed to one another like the pieces of a simple puzzle. I marveled at each plastic innard as though it had a life of its own. The bubble gum stomach, a dozing piglet, shaded itself under the liver's burgundy fedora. The pancreas beamed a lemon yellow. The uterus was transparent, and plopped like a ball bearing into the pelvic basin. The last item was always the small intestine, furrowed like the brain, only dumber, I knew. It clacked like a domino when I fit it into the remaining cavity in the abdomen. Then, presto, there she was: Madonna of the bodily baubles. An idealization of our entrails.

Sometimes when I visualize my interior, I see something like an inverted night sky, a galactic depth where vain spirits wail and rhapsodize. These chimera twinkle like constellations, deities from a bygone time. Yet the world laid open by the surgeon's scalpel is pure gore, an arrangement of wet, blood-colored sacs, each barely distinguishable from the next. Had I been able to be present at Susan's surgery, had I peered into Susan's open belly, I would have found an inarticulate and ruddy mass of viscera. I would have searched for Susan, for her tenderness, her spunk, and would have discovered only those slippery gizzards we all share.

The sight of our guts insults the mysterious divas inside us. Who are those souls who sing high above our wiggling cells? What are they made of? Do they simply plummet like kites when cells no longer keep them aloft? And what remains of their songs?

■ ■ ■

All the great music of the world is prompted by desire. I'm reminded of a young Billie Holiday, her tomboy voice poking up like a crocus from the earth of Ben Webster's sax: *If my heart could only talk, heaven would be mine.*

If our hearts could only talk—and they do, they sing a paean to strange bedfellows: lust and exaltation. They sing orgasms in the temple, epiphanies in the bedroom. They sing the groin's psalm, the spirit's fever. They sing to be outside the Earth's time, where bodies blaze steadily like stars.

■ ■ ■

December, approaching Christmas. Susan recuperates, and we spend days cooking. We surround ourselves with the reassuring odors of lemon peel, mulling spices, roasted nuts. Our senses cast us from fearsome bodies and restore us to bodies that are home. We gorge ourselves with spoonfuls of batter, satin ropes of chocolate, broken tiles of shortbread.

On Christmas Eve I go with Susan to church. In spite of my past as a heathen, I try to be open. This is All Saints Episcopal, one of the most progressive Episcopal churches in the country. They provide emergency aid to refugees, feed the homeless, perform gay unions; the least I can do is sit politely and ponder this faith.

The church itself is gorgeous, festooned with fragrant garlands of juniper and cedar. The musk of the forest is heightened by the smell of burning resin, of frankincense. A chamber orchestra plays a concerto by Scarlatti. So far, I like it.

The minister begins by talking about birth, about our being reborn this night through the story of Jesus. I brace myself. It's a pitch, an opportunity to lure the newcomer into the fold. He wants me to surrender, to lose myself in an orgasm of the Lord.

I don't belong here, this church full of families, all apparently innocent of doubt, each trading their moments of piety for a claim in the hereafter. I look at the cross and see crusades, inquisitions, dark ages. I see grown men and women warming their backs while their children burn as heretics. I see missionaries and plagues of syphilis, measles, alcoholism. . . .

Then the songs work their magic on me. First there's "Silent Night" by Franz Grüber, rising and falling like respiration. I relax. During "Hark the Herald Angels Sing" I feel like weeping, weeping for the fragile entity that is Susan and me, weeping for the tenacious beauty of this song, which will outlive us both. Mostly, I'm pining for the vanishing moment itself.

The minister tells the story of Christmas. I mentally translate the words of his sermon into a pagan language, a broader metaphor that will contain my own vision of spiritual life. Observance of the solstice is analogous to the star/child's appearance in the night. Light is our divine element, the ember's glow from the Bang's maelstrom, the last shimmer of Eminence. We are made of it ourselves. This, I conclude, must be how the Jesus thing works: to give energy a human face.

I work my way in and out of the minister's sermon. Occasionally I'm stumped by phrases that simply don't translate into my religion, that seem fixed in his dogma, nailed down, as it were. Like "Everlasting life through Jesus Christ." Finally he invites us to come forward and take communion. This is to be my intimate moment with Jesus. And though music has provided the perfect foreplay, I can't guarantee I'll swoon.

But the music continues to erode my defenses. "Angels We Have Heard on High." The chorus savors exaltation, elongates it. *Glo-o-o-o-ria.* The word is liquefied, sung like extended laughter, the notes tumbling over themselves. By the last chorus all the stops on the organ are out and the bass notes nearly shake my lungs. Now the word *Gloria,* once tumbling like a stream, is an all-out torrent, into which I'm swept. Don't I yearn for something more durable than my bleak little parcel of time? Lord, won't some chariot lift this singer far from the obsolescence of her body, far from cells already conspiring in disaster?

I want to taste the spiritual body, to run its blood over my tongue. I approach the altar like a child, ready to suspend disbelief. A large blond woman in a white robe beams at me. "This is the body of Our Lord." I'm filled with gratitude as she places what appears to be a miniature coaster into my palm. Then a man in a white robe holds a silver chalice in his right hand, just out of reach. "This is the blood of Our Lord, Jesus Christ." I can't reach the chalice. When he sees my confusion he is impatient and barks, "Just dip the wafer into the cup!" He means into the smaller cup in his *left* hand. The grandeur of the moment is paling fast. I peer down into the silver eye cup. The sacred blood is clear, beyond anemic. The man's hair looks greasy and I feel ashamed to be on my knees. I coat the tip of the wafer with the Boone's Farm and pop it into my mouth.

■ ■ ■

Was it childish to expect the spiritual to pique the senses? to hope the mysteries of the universe would reveal themselves through the medium of flavor? Even the starches in the most stoic and simple cracker turn to sugar on my tongue. Yet this wafer clung, unyielding, never betraying a hint of sweetness, changing only from parched to gummy. And the wine, the few molecules that stowed themselves away in the pores of that wafer, seasoned the paste enough to make it faintly medicinal.

Why would this ritual food, this morsel sauced with garlands, incense, and a choir, be so bland, so difficult to swallow?

I had to contain myself from howling with cynicism as I stood and walked back to the pews. The insipid taste of Jesus brought me back to myself. I am a dyke, mammal of homoerotic persuasion, a soul anchored to a twat. My life will not outlast the forces of entropy, I will be reborn only among microbes, or possibly, though not probably, through the curves and serifs of these words.

As we left the church I had never felt such homesickness for the crass world of matter. I craved crusty bread washed down with purple Syrah. I lusted for the realm of the palpable: Susan's heat, the softness of her breasts, the salt of her skin. I was more resolute than ever that only my senses best teach me how to live.

Yet each night we lay together I pray this happiness won't be taken from me.

See, I can't escape my lapses into hocus-pocus, the childlike grasping at wishes.

An older Billie Holiday floods up this time, a woman in the last years of her life. *In time the Rockies may crumble, Gibraltar may tumble. They're only made of clay. . . .* Though worn and corroded, her voice retains its tomboy swagger, and Ben Webster's sax still breathes beside her, earthy as ever.

JOURNEY TO THE
CENTER OF THE EARTH

When I was nine I went to see the movie *Journey to the Center of the Earth*. I had gone expressly to ogle my heartthrob, Pat Boone. I don't know what it was, apart from his pillowy voice, that drew me to him, enticing me into the dark of the Coronet Theater. Perhaps it was narcissism, pure and simple; his face was apple-cheeked, prepubescent, like my own.

I'd like to say I'm a different person than I was then, subject to only the most sophisticated attractions. That I'd rather play strip poker with the pope than have to gawk at those apple cheeks ever again. But I'm learning that the heart stockpiles its many quirky affinities, the way compost still stows away some aspect of last year's cantaloupe, and that embarrassment for any past love is pure futility. The composition of my heart is, alas, less the grand stuff of art, and more the dross contained in a child's pocket: a Speidel bracelet, a troll doll with lime green hair, some polished stones.

At any rate, whatever puerile twinges lured me to *Journey to the Center of the Earth*, they were quickly forgotten once the special effects danced onto my retina. Rivers of magma shimmered like lamé as Pat Boone and his band of explorers traversed the subterranean realm of caves, streams and lava floes. Ancient reptiles reared their ugly heads and flashed their sets of pointy incisors. The watery vortex at the center of the earth funneled into some other reality. And I knew one thing after the lights in the Coronet came up. I wanted to go there, down, straight to the very core.

■ ■ ■

Some thirty years later I traveled through the caves of Southwestern France. Once upon a time ancient rivers surged through the region of the Périgord, scooping out valleys and boring tunnels through soft breaks in the limestone. Caves were left in the wake of that frenzy. And soon people—for in time human beings had migrated to those valleys—found their way inside them.

Water also left accretions of calcite and other minerals within those chambers. Everywhere that water had dripped or drooled, scales formed. Some residues jutted like nipples, others sagged like dewlaps. Over time these formations resembled the musculature of animals, monstrous flowers, and fantastic, incomprehensible architecture. Hallucinations lay dormant within that rock, and with them, religion. Under the flicker of torchlight, cosmologies began to live within those deposits, worlds were taking shape.

From the parking lot the Gouffre de Padirac looks nothing like my notion of a cave. It is simply an enormous hole in the ground, fringed with brush. Moss slobbers from the lip like a wet chamois. I take an elevator to the bottom of that hole, where I'm met by a boatman, a pale, bowlegged Frenchman who poles his flatboat through the waters of this underworld like Charon.

Gliding with the subterranean river, it's easy to envision the forces that created the nether world. The crystal waters still gouge concavities, and driblets are patiently sculpting eccentric spires. To this day formations fool the mind. Here milk surges over a tower of plates. There, batter oozes from the lip of a bowl in lustrous ribbons. You'd think this artwork required a shutter speed of 1000, rather than a time-lapse spanning the centuries. "Look above you," the boatman whispers, "see ze elephant? see eets trunk ahnd ears?"

Though water is always seeking the lowest level, its deposits often rise upward to defy gravity. As I peer up at stalactites, those sinewy gewgaws readily transform themselves into gargoyles. It's easy to imagine how these ornate dungeons evolved into cathedrals.

It is theorized that Paleolithic people gathered in these caves to perform sacred activities. In this valley alone, paintings adorn the walls of as many as sixty caves. Depictions of an array of animal species, many now extinct, graze, buck and gallop within the ochre limestone.

My favorite is in the cave of Pech-Merle. A painting of two horses is situated on a rock face, itself resembling the profile of a horse. The horses, one facing left, the other, right, are overlapped at the hind quarters. It's as though the same horse had simply pivoted, ready to bolt in any direction. Pigment mixed with saliva and spat onto the wall has airbrushed spots on these animals. This technique has also stenciled the artist's hands, a repeated signature floating above the horses. Palms press against the surface of stone, they are greetings from another era, a benediction.

Were these paintings magical invocations? Declarations of ownership? Scenery for ritual theater? Art for art's sake? Whatever function they might have served is anyone's guess. One thing is certain, the art of the Paleolithic period is darned good—more energetic than anything Europe will experience for another sixteen thousand years—and the caves themselves, safe from weather, temperate year-round, even hypoallergenic, make ideal galleries.

Nearby, up the road from the site where Cro-Magnon man was found, the cave of le Grand Roc boasts chambers with crystalline, appliquéed ceilings. Alcoves glitter with tiny Baccarat needles. Fissures in the rock are honeycombed with spangles. It's Pluto's jewelry box, Nature's foppery, a bangle overlooking a valley of bones.

■ ■ ■

Metamorphic rock is often a diorama of colorful abstraction, a stilled pond I want to take the time to explore—like jasper, with its oil lamp jumbles of color, or moss agate, with its green tendrils suspended in silicon gel. For me, art always takes a second place to my collection of rocks. The random abstractions of Morris Louis or Jackson Pollock seem to me to plagiarize the rich chaos embedded in my stones. Some minerals, like scheelite, shine under a UV lamp, but far better than if Helen Frankenthaler had taken LSD and gone Day-Glo. And moonstone glows of its own eerie volition, more luminous than Rothko.

An igneous rock is regurgitated directly from the Earth's smelter. The earth burps up lava, spits up feldspar, quartz, granite. Magma is the torch we've carried from creation, the crucible bearing a smattering of the sun. You can almost hear the godlike roar in the black eye of obsidian, the squeals of steam released from lava's pores.

Sedimentary rocks are formed in silence. Mute collections of dandruff, pollen, insect wings, you name it, quietly conspire to bury us, blanket after heavy blanket. There's no use in trying to resist it. The earth's crust will seduce us; it is a parfait, a torte. Last year's layer of powdered sugar becomes today's brittle sheet of toffee. How sweet to go down into that stillness like a dozing trilobite, how delicious.

The antennae of alien lobsters are etched into sandstone, the freakish smiles of infraterrestrials frozen within shale. Organisms who would otherwise have gone down into obscurity are fixed in the mud, like actors whose footprints hardened in the pavement at Grauman's.

■ ■ ■

I'd like to think of my dreams as sunken treasure, master-pieces obscured by the dross of wakeful, daily life. However, the images I cough up from the subterranea of dream life are, more often than not, cluttered and forgettable, littered with tourists from Cable Access and *People* magazine. Like a good cook, the mind uses whatever is in the cupboard. Then, voilà! Tonight on ze menu we have . . . last year's cantaloupe for starters, a troll doll sketched onto limestone, a flatboat poled by an hebetic movie star.

I can sometimes make myself fall asleep by trying to discon-nect my thoughts, letting the filaments untie themselves—each loose end languishing into a curlicue, a fine net that unravels—until dreams, like small creatures in a stream, wash through. But most of the time if I'm away from my lover, I've found it difficult to surrender to sleep without the buzz of her snores. It's more than just the mantra of those purring adenoids, of course. There's the smell of her hair, and the reassurance of her silhouette across the pillow.

How different one's face is when sleeping! Susan's face is not exactly her own. She is somewhere underneath that face, deep inside the brain of the ancient lizard, doing push-ups in the thalamus. She is rising and falling with the rumba, the umbra, the calypso. She's onboard the *Niña,* the *Pinta* and the medulla oblongata. The New World waves to her from the insides of her eyelids. Of course, she is the New World as well. Sometimes her hands paddle the sheets like a crocodile, sometimes her teeth chatter like castanets.

Look, down and down she goes. Where is that depth so close to death? The dieback of winter turns gangbusters by spring, a confirmation that, for some at least, death is only a kind of slumber. The gods of sleep and death, Hypnos and Thanatos, were mythic brothers—the cave bear's Romulus and Remus, suckling and slurping in the den. Is she safe in there with them, all alone in the deep?

■ ■ ■

Pluto's palace, at last! Its domes are spiraling like an enormous nautilus. The ocean, if you listen for it, breathes at this entrance, sounding like the snoring of so many sleeping, sibilant souls. Beds clutter these hallways, and wax from candelabras, accrued through millennia, climbs from the floor like stalagmites. Of their own volition, the tubes of hookahs rise, cobras bobbing to an invisible charmer. Where is your host? You hear him pacing. You hear him sighing. Will you never see his face?

Finally. *She* has arrived! She is called Persephone, Eurydice, Sleeping Beauty, Kore.

Her room has been waiting for her. You caught a glimpse of it before she was escorted inside. It is ornamented with the flesh of pomegranate. Each rubicund seed has been rubbed warm and shiny. And the bed, a water bed, is strewn with animal pelts, and latex.

You took pity on her at first. Poor innocent girl, you thought. You were, of course, crying for your own innocence. For when you listened, ears pressed against the juicy, mosaic door, you were aghast. You'd expected to hear the mournful sobbing of a homesick daughter. Instead you heard salacious moans, the whir of vibrators, and playful, teasing, laughter. . . .

When he finally left her chamber, most of the candles in the hallway had burned out. Much of him was in shadow. But as he neared the last sputtering candle at the end of the hall, wisps of his mohair sweater caught the candlelight like the corona of an eclipse, and you could see his figure briefly, and brilliantly, illuminated. He is a giant. But that is only the half of it. As he turned at the end of the hall, you glimpsed something else— how his ass was as bare as the moon. And it was not a man's ass you saw, more of a . . . fanny really, a ripe soft thing that swayed, left and right, as his feathery chaps shushed into the dark, and he was gone.

Any day now Dionysus, Orpheus and Demeter will be coming down to reclaim her, whistling "Dixie," whistling in the dark, whistling to fear no evil, whistling in the shadow of the valley of death.

Of course coming down here is one thing, you've proven that. But getting back up is yet quite another. In the first place one must do it blindfolded, blind as a mole, as a worm, as anything that has forgone the light of day. But, of course, they do it, undaunted, every year. Jumping rivulets of fire, inching rock ledges, sidestepping sleeping Godzilla. And ofttimes with the girl scratching and kicking to be let go.

And finally, when they get her home, they'll try what they can to deprogram her. Sleep deprivation for starters, a mug of joe, an incandescent bulb that stays on for weeks, and a good chilling douse of common sense. This is what life is all about, they'll say: seeds, harvest, the making of new life. Wake up, Persephone. You once were dead, but now you liveth!

■ ■ ■

Who are those oracles of NPR, Bob Edwards, Susan Stamberg and Carl Castle if not Orpheus, Demeter and Dionysus in disguise? By the time I've silenced my alarm clock, their reportage has put leagues between me and the underworld.

Dreams? Who can remember them? When I retrieve the fragments, they are shredded and disconnected, like a souvenir matchbook I've salvaged, too late, from the washing machine.

It is a virtue to sleep less in our culture. One desires ways to become, like the Adventists' magazine, *Awake!* Cities like New York and Rome are predicated on caffeine. Everywhere jackhammers are pounding, briefcases are swinging. Cappuccino makers whine, the milk froths, and children dance under hydrants spouting methamphetamine.

Headlines are bringing you up-to-date. Bosses want every-thing ASAP. Even the gurus advise you to Be Here Now. So why is it that each night we are dragged into our beds, forced to lie still and forget our days? Who is this kidnapper who holds us captive one-third of all our lives?

■ ■ ■

The universe is cooling, we're told. What once was brilliant and unified is slowly dissipating, curdling into motes. But let's not throw in the towel just yet. In spite of all those doors slam-ming in the cosmos, there is regeneration. I'm not talking karma or mummies or Seth. Look, right this minute there are sow bugs out there, trundling through my compost bin, worms digesting their way through leftovers. And even though people are laid out like corpses in their beds, the cells of their brains are regrouping, charging up like AA batteries. Synapses are forming unholy unions, illegal partnerships. Equations are trading their unknown quantities. And something fresh will come of it.

Rock-a-bye, baby, in the treetops.

Susan is down the hall wrapped in our bed, charging her bat-teries. Her uvula is thrumming my all-time favorite lullaby. Our bed equals the smell of her hair, which equals trust, therefore the peace to free-fall into X, that den where twins are sucking dark milk.

When the bough breaks, the cradle will fall . . .

Once upon a time a dreaming scientist perceived the benzene molecule as a snake eating its own tail. That was an unholy union equaling a bit of luck. With any luck of my own, I might dredge up a treasure tonight. Will it be sapphires or Speidel?

Pat, oh Pat, with your rosy cheeks and your green hair a-flowin', take me down that river. Show me the way.

. . . and down will come baby, cradle and all.

BUGABOO IN THE AMERICAN MUSEUM OF NATURAL HISTORY

Undoubtedly philosophers are in the right when they tell us that nothing is great or little otherwise than by comparison. It might have pleased fortune to let the Lilliputians find some nation where the people were as diminutive with respect to them as they were to me.

—Jonathan Swift, *Gulliver's Travels*

Let's move over to the park, Peter suggested, the trees are turning. We walked swiftly, like New Yorkers, down Amsterdam Avenue. I was trying to catch my breath while my brother strode breezily, his eyes alive with the street's flurry. In his midfifties, Peter had recently moved to New York and never looked better. He was at the height of his powers, just itching to make this colossal city his own. With each block he pointed out his new foraging spots: this one for espresso, that for fish.

Besides the gene of our blondness and a familial reverence for teasing, my brother and I share a passion for food and a love of nature. So it's no wonder that, after lunch at his favorite oyster bar, we sped back uptown to the American Museum of Natural History, to spend the afternoon.

One foot in the door of the museum and the street was

forgotten. However much Manhattan may have ignited our imaginations, the dinosaur skeletons in the entry hall and their invocation of Carboniferous forests opened us to unpeopled vistas, stretches of geological time.

The skeleton models toyed with my sense of scale. It's common knowledge how reptiles—like the blue-bellied lizards of my youth, the ones I nabbed as they did their push-ups on the patio—were once the biggest things to walk the planet. But standing next to the towering Allosaurus, mid-size as dinosaurs go, his stature was anything but hackneyed. I could easily imagine his agility, his ferocity, his aptitude for making me dessert.

My brother and I were still savoring the sensations brought on by our imaginary encounter with the dinosaurs, when we came upon a plastic model of a mosquito seventy-five times its actual size. Both Peter and I suffer from bug fear. We freak out at the sight of wobbly antennae, segmented limbs, and those fingerlike appendages that flutter around the mouths of bugs, called palpi. My brother and I share this condition more than anyone else in our family and certainly more than anyone else I know. So when I tell you that we stumbled across this monument of a bug, and were stunned by both fear and fascination, frozen as though eye to eye with Medusa, you get the idea.

We were spellbound as well by the artistry of the model: every hair, every vein, every scale was in its place. Bulging compound eyes, like charred cauliflowers, signaled an altogether alien intelligence. Antennae sprung from its head like two dead Christmas trees. The creature had, I thought, a kind of jouster's design, an outfit for a medieval siege. Hooks jutted from its feet. The wiry angular legs were plated with brittle rust-colored skirts. Protrusions resembling iron maces jutted from under the wings, in what might, in some broad stretch of imagination, be called armpits. The crowning glory, the poised proboscis, ran down the middle of two hairy shafts like a built-in jousting rod.

The model was a work of art, like the slap of a Zen master,

both in its unflinching accuracy and in its ability to alter perception. "Wouldn't it be amazing to live with something like this?" I asked, dazzled for the moment by this plastic object behind Plexiglas. Of course I could no sooner live with that behemoth than with a photo blowup of Jeffrey Dahmer. Either would inject ice into my veins, subject me to a world in which human sympathies mean zip. Peter replied, "I'd be scared shitless." I looked into his eyes and laughed, warmed by our similarity.

When did it begin, this phobia of half the world's living things? Before the age of seven, bugs were as fascinating to me as birds or lizards. I had once hunted grasshoppers for fish bait with the nonchalance of one gathering dandelions. Grasshoppers looked like Old World gentlemen with their high starched collars and long waistcoats. I had excavated ant mounds, my shovel unearthing the nurseries until I struck buried treasure, the cache of sand-size grubs. Was I nervous about all the ants in a frenzy at my feet? Was I fazed by the grasshopper spittle on my fingers? What must it have been like to live in that little girl's Eden, to exist without repulsion of things creepy and crawly? I must have been under a spell, mesmerized by the sound of wings searing the air, caressed by spindly legs. I might have allowed spiders to hobble across my fingers, pill bugs to mingle in the forest of my scalp. The thought that I once existed without a terror of bugs makes me retroactively panicked, as though I were confronting a history of unsafe sex.

Shortly before I turned seven I scurried around our garden with a small net, scooping the air for moths and butterflies. The few creatures I nabbed I carried back to my room and smothered with a wad of cotton soaked in chloroform. Then I pinned the corpses inexpertly to blocks of Styrofoam, where they hung, crucified, paper-thin trophies.

I enjoyed my new hobby until I found the giant moth in the swimming pool, its wing span nearly five inches wide. Carrying the creature back to my room, I felt the world shift on its axis. I no longer saw its wings banded with chestnut, cream and coal, or marked with spots that looked like owl's eyes. I beheld only its churlish body, as though its fluted belly and funnel-shaped mouth were equal in size to my own. The moth was instantly grotesque. I abandoned it in our fireplace as though it were a soiled tissue. When I returned to my room, the other creatures in my collection seemed less like gossamer angels, more like leathery Martians—their Technicolor wings barely a distraction from their new monstrosity.

Since then all bugs are horrid. While I might decry the ferocity of a bear as magnificent, the very structure of a gnat's mouth will send me up a tree. Where are its lips? Its tongue?

When I say bugs I mean all arthropods. Isn't this the nature of prejudice, that it will blur distinctions? As far as I'm concerned, they're all alike: the flying, crawling six-legged insects, as well as the arachnids, the centipedes, even the crustaceans. Yes, even crawdads, the critters I also stalked in my childhood as I roamed creek beds in my high-tops. What is a crayfish if not a mole cricket with pinchers? A scorpion without a stinger? It ambles like a bug, feeds like a bug. It has wobbly antennae, maxillary palpi. It's an arthropod, through and through, therefore: bug.

Likewise, crab. Crab used to be delightful, interactive food, something you had to break open to enjoy, the geode of the animal kingdom. The shell was Chinese red, and once cracked, you could fish out the snowy meat, saline, sweet, and squeaky clean.

One night in a restaurant the sight of a crab repulsed me. It ceased to signal festivity, only horror. The crab was placed before me, whole, steamed, belly up, like an enormous spider in a suit of armor. The sections of its underside were scored with pale hairs, and the contraption that was its mouth, also hairy, seemed more akin to the trap door of an alien spaceship. The crab's flesh, once feathery and sweet, now threatened me with the willies. I had to send it back to the kitchen.

I'm an entomophobe. I feel I would perish if I let a bug larger than an aspirin walk on my hand. When I go to buy cat food at For Pets Only, I keep a safe distance from the terrariums where the tarantulas are kept. If I glimpse photographs of bugs in a book, I'll quickly flip the pages to avoid them. The forms of bugs are shocking to me, psychologically *verboten*. I can't bring myself to consider them, like a fundamentalist who averts her eyes in the presence of striptease.

Bugs house all the traits I reject. Into them I have projected all the spurned, shadowy attributes of humankind. They seem to me to be cold-hearted, unscrupulous, fascistic. They work too hard. Their battles are too bloodthirsty. Where is their sentimentality?

■ ■ ■

Asterisks on the page; bacillus in the body. An amoeba, a virus, a critter inciting Montezuma's revenge. Larger, plural and visible to the eye, they're lousy in the scalp, the pubis, or the bed. Some are psychosomatic, cooties that make your skin crawl. When in the works, they're a defect or imperfection, a gremlin in the engine, something bogus on the hard drive. A bug can be a small microphone, hidden from view, gumming up the works, fouling privacy, threatening peace.

Then one is bugged as one might be by a swarm of gnats, an onslaught of scabies, a persistent thought, a persistent thought. It's an obsession or a craze, like something your system can't throw off, like something that drives you in spite of yourself. To be bugged is to be insane, given to crazes, the world up to its ears in cooties; to land in the insane asylum, bughouse, looking into the bug-eyed face of your bugaboos, bugbears, bogeyman.

On the bright side, the bugger, the jiggie-boo, gives us jitterbug, bugaloo, boogie-woogie, ants in our pants, bees in our bonnets. In other words, something's delicious, in fact, necessary in what may, at first, seem strange. Mutation and diversity keep life at its fittest. Anomaly is the vermin's forte, and history is in their corner. And that's why, even with a megaton of DDT or tetracycline, we'll never rid the world of bugs. Never.

■ ■ ■

So what's the fuss? Look closely at a corpse and you'll see the swarms roiling in its tissues. They have no respect, look how they cluster at the lips of starving children. See how they deposit their eggs into the sores of the sick. They are agents of decomposition, annihilation of all we hold dear.

Even the most vital of us are composed of mindless hordes. Multitudes swarm in the cockles of my anus, in the sea of my spit. Armies of immunity are in a standoff with armies of infection. Apocalypse is in abeyance, until one day the cellular fortress begins to crumble and disease takes hold. Of course, there are a few friendly tenants inside me, critters chowing down in my intestines, converting Monday's pasta into dung.

But, by and large, they have no regard for personal boundaries. They crawl over my threshold, amble across my table. There's little I can do to persuade them otherwise. I'm reminded of how the world is not really dominated by a human sensibility. Impudent flies keck on my window ledge. Earwigs steadily encroach, squatters under my carpet. Moths plunder bits of my wardrobe, and daddy longlegs appropriate my bedroom after dark, giving me pause before I reach to turn out the light.

Insects have a ringside seat at diabolism, staring into the chainsaw mandibles of larger invertebrates, or into the gaping shears of whole armies. A spider, Lizzy Borden with six eyes, paralyzes her victim and lays her eggs inside its body. Or the mantis eats the brain of her lover while making him perform the nasty. This is creepy sci-fi stuff, not even the pedestrian kind of predation we can expect from the most ferocious of mammals.

On the other hand, bugs are the world's seraphim. They

most closely enjoy heaven, crawling into the calyxes of flowers, probing wells of nectar, gnawing the perfect edges of leaves. Insects and flowers enjoy a symbiosis, seem as inseparable as toast and jam; but this was not always so.

Insects crept on the planet millions of years before the appearance of flowers. Silverfish, those starch eaters who thrive under leaf litter and conspire to gobble up this very page, are Devonian inventions, older than dinosaurs, and longer lasting. Like the dinosaurs, the first insects feasted on leaves, on debris, or on one another. Flowers snuck on the scene much later, dressing themselves up to seduce the curiosity of bugs, to ensnare their incomparable noses, to taunt their multiple eyes. Like billboards, blossoms now loom and sway in the bugscape, REST STOP, FOOD — NEXT EXIT.

Imagine our planet four hundred million years ago: the world is in the grip of an ice age, the long reign of the trilobites is in decline. Finally the proto-continent, Gondwana, drifts away from the South Pole, its glaciers melt, and the seas rise once more. Fish begin to colonize the waters, and the trilobite's cousin, the once outnumbered crustacean flourishes. On the land, amid mosses and incipient ferns, scorpions and tiny wormlike segmented bugs make their momentous odyssey onto the mud. A scant hundred million years later, by the Carboniferous, forests of tree ferns tower over cockroaches and silverfish routing in leaf litter. Proto spiders spin their silks, and dragonflies with two-foot wingspans rattle the air.

Since then four cataclysmic events, probably meteorite impacts, caused worldwide climatic upheavals and extinctions of most of the world's species. Somehow, through the ice and ash, the tsunamis and acid rains, bugs crept through the gates of each new world to prosper and multiply, to recreate themselves along with the new habitat.

In their mouth parts, segmented legs and bulging eyes I experience the Devonian, me-first Zeitgeist. Theirs is a world oblivious to maternal cooing and sibling affection. They will seize any opportunity, will not take no for an answer. Like panic, they are the stuff of primordial survival. In their hisses and chirps I hear the shrill scream of the medulla oblongata, ungagged. Just visceral, skin-crawling emotion, strictly glandular stuff, not a trace of the heroic.

And let's face it, they look weird. Bug design didn't draw its first breath from this Cenozoic world. They have no bones, only the brittle cuticle of their exoskeletons. They have no lungs, but breathe through openings along the sides of their bodies. Their blood doesn't circulate oxygen. Their mouths, which vary from species to species, are made up of parts that include lips, jaws, palpi, and some combination of tools, resembling in human terms, scissors, tweezers, saws, straws, fingers, fangs, syringes, harpoons or—as in the case of dragonflies' mouths—cranes.

It's more than just their alien bodies, though, that spook me. Even with its head riding eight whorling legs, an octopus's two eyes mirror my own. I recognize a familiar brain. With bugs I find creatures whose heads are honeycombed with eyes, whose faces refract my stare. The bug is a saboteur, trying to undermine my frame of reference.

■ ■ ■

Susan, my better half, and I are driving through the Cotes de Rhône to visit the house of the nature writer Henri Fabre. Small tractors heaped with purple grapes bounce along the shoulders of the road. The afternoon sun gilds the vineyards in broad bands that alternate with blue shadows. The air is sizzling with the songs of cicadas. Fabre tells us in *The Life of the Grasshopper* how the Provençal peasants say the cicada is singing, *"Sego, sego, sego!"* ("Reap, reap, reap!"). We approach another truck laden with purple treasure, and the grizzled farmer at the wheel waves to us as we pass.

As we near Fabre's house, now a museum, I am thinking of his observations on the praying mantis, whose behaviors, particularly whose mating habits, appalled even him.

> The male, absorbed in the performance of his vital functions, holds the female in a tight embrace. But the wretch has no head; he has no neck; he has hardly a body. The other, with her muzzle turned over her shoulder, continues very placidly to gnaw what remains of the gentle swain. And, all the time, that masculine stump, holding on firmly, goes on with the business!

I've seen a photograph of Fabre's study, cluttered with jars and displays. What monsters will I find there, mounted and framed on those walls? or pickled in jars? Giant beetles with rhinoceros horns? Treehoppers with stegosaurus backs? Or perhaps even the "tigress" herself, the "ogress in ambush," a green praying mantis?

We pull up to the iron gate and it is locked, *fermé*. I peek through the hedges. The evening air glows like butter and thrums with the movements of a thousand wings. I feel disappointed to have missed the opportunity to visit the home of this most lyrical of nature writers—this teacher who had the gall to admit girl students into his classroom nearly a century ago. I feel relieved as well, though it may be years before I'll be back, to be spared the probable confrontation with his collection of bugs.

That night we eat in our tiny hotel. A German family is at one table, monks from the nearby seminary are at the other. I'm curious about these young acolytes. Years ago I, too, had an interest in religion. I was in the midst of a love affair, dizzy with quixotic emotion, and felt it was possible to embrace the whole of life in my ardor. Mistaking libido for something much greater, I saw myself as a latent mystic. I was in my twenties, still young enough to believe I had the potential to become anything, so it was with great sadness that, in time, I realized the sham. Love with a capital *L* is not informed by a love for one, and—big incidental here—I would never, never in a million years be able to connect with insects. My capacity to love, to embrace the totality of life, was stunted by secular passions and tenacious fears.

Susan and I finish our dinner, return to our room, and as I emerge from the bathroom Susan exclaims that there's a giant bug on the curtain near the open window. The curtains are a floral green print and it's hard for me to perceive anything on them other than stylized vines and swollen blossoms. Then I'm seized with panic as the form of a LARGE praying mantis emerges. My fear is contagious, because Susan, usually a pro in matters of insect removal, now hasn't the stomach to transport it to the open window. We scurry back up to the dining room and convince our waiter to help us remove the *mante religieuse*. He obviously thinks we are urban wimps, but is polite nevertheless, and follows us down to our room. I lock myself in the bathroom, completely at the mercy of my fear, while Susan and the young man accomplish the unthinkable. They encourage the mantis to abandon her refuge of the curtain and exit via the open window. *Vite! vite!* the Frenchman purrs as he tosses the thing into the dark.

I am a creature fourteen times the size of the *mante*, one hundred times more powerful. My withdrawal into the bathroom is comparable to a hammerhead shark fleeing from a minnow. The bug, she may be smaller, but the fear, she is big.

Three days later in Florence we learn from Italian television that the Rhône valley near Henri Fabre's house had been scoured by a flood. I feel utterly silly to have been so cowed, when real catastrophe had been close at our heels.

Let's say for the sake of those young monks, for the sake of the mystic I once imagined myself to be, for the sake of Love with a capital *L,* that we are descended from bugs. Let's say our antennae evolved into the cerebral cortex, that the febrile sensors of the exterior world grew into an organ of language. Let's say we can still feel two more sets of shoulders along our ribs, that in dreams our phantom limbs continue to stroke the air. That each night we strain to remember how our wings unfold from their casings. We are Gregor Samsa in reverse, beetles who awaken to a giant's world of adipose tissue, red blood, Dr. Martens, fiber optics, free will.

How do our bug-selves negotiate the hominid's convulsions? Why were we reduced to this world of limited appendages— only two, max, of everything, and no more? Why has the world dimmed to pale chromatics, no hue more intense than red or violet? Where is the bouquet in the nectar? Why have our mouths been brought up too short, too few parts with which to tear and suck? How, being at such a deficit, will we ever manage to crawl through the gate, into the next new world?

■ ■ ■

After leaving the mosquito, my brother and I found ourselves in the Hall of Meteorites. From a distance those hunkering monoliths seemed anything but mind-boggling. But close up, and with the help of some nearby text, the meteorites gave us a sense of past time so plumbless we felt dizzy as we tried to imagine the violent narrative that brought them from the core of one planetary body to the crust of our own. They were time travelers, pelting the sky from a depth only measurable in millennia. Yet, sawed in half, those iron chunks looked nickel plated, bright as newly minted Susan B. Anthonys.

Like Gulliver, whose relative height allowed him to piss on the tiny palace of Lilliput, and later is nearly impaled by the stings of giant wasps in the kingdom of Brobdingnag, I was jostled between big and small, small and big. I remembered Gulliver's statement that "nothing is great or little otherwise than by comparison." I felt foolish to have had the arrogance to assume I knew the difference, like thinking that because I see the sun rise and set, it revolves around the earth.

Compared to the tumultuous eons survived by these rocks, who were we? I was thinking not only of my brother and me, but of the whole cotton-pickin' shebang: the human race, the age of mammals, the history of all living things. My mind squirmed. I felt myself to be in the presence of something alien and ghastly. It palpated me and found me unsuitable. It regarded me with one of its immense compound eyes. I felt squeamish to be such a tiny speck under the scrutiny of the Incomprehensible.

Before we left, in the Hall of Human Evolution, Peter and I saw a diorama representing two prehistoric hominids on the Tanzanian savanna. In the background, an explosive volcano has blanketed the ground with pale ash. The naked couple move together, his arm around her shoulder, their eyes scanning their new, merciless surroundings. They are searching for a trace of the familiar, their faces reflecting disbelief. I couldn't shake the simplicity of their physical touch, a gesture of comfort and shared experience.

At closing time Peter and I headed for the exit, as near to each other as the two represented in the tableau. The museum was filled with creatures like ourselves, children, women and men, each as captured by the private drama of individual struggle as the next, each the center of a universe, each to be outlived in too short a time, too coldly, too brutally. A look of fondness passed between us as we moved through the dusk blue doorway, into the city's trumpets, into that fragile light.

CLOVEN HOOVES &
DEVILED HAMS

An angel is a soul who has not grown sufficiently.

—Sufi Master Khan

Since I was old enough to stay up beyond 10 P.M., I've been a fan of horror films, especially the old films, the black and white melodramas, finding in their shadowy Gothic interiors the archetypes for my childhood horrors. Vampires and werewolves lurched through the tulle fog of my young psyche, making their beds each dawn, awakening refreshed each night. These were stylized monsters, stripped of detail or color, opaque creatures upon whom I could attach my fears. Horror films, thanks to the theatrical glower of Boris Karloff, or the Kabuki poses of Bela Lugosi, had been cathartic.

Like most children's spooks, my monsters were hatched by my parents' shortcomings: Dad, two sheets to the wind, turned downright sinister, and Ma, trying to control what she could not, got witchier by the minute. However, my hellions lived, not within my parents' bedroom, nor with any of my cast of foibled grown-ups, but inside the recesses of my closet. Each night I'd lie in terror, nearly certain of a soft chiming of hangers. Inside, hunched among my coats and blouses, a werewolf or a vampire licked his chops, breathed his breath. He waited to fling open my closet door like a wraith sprung from Pandora's box. My only defense, I rationalized, would be my innocence of him. If I could make *him* believe I had no knowledge of him, could convince *him* of my blissful slumber, he would be powerless and I would be safe. My nights were spent laboring with an appearance of sleep. Of course, this compulsion only perpetuated itself, making me only more aware of Evil, less convinced of innocence.

When I was in my early twenties I went with two friends to see a movie about demonic possession. There had been considerable hype about the film, stories of crew members encountering bizarre accidents on the set, or of people in the audience having convulsions during a screening. It was touted as a movie that would scare the bejesus out of you. So of course we were dying to go. We waited in a long line that coiled around the block. When we finally raced down the aisle of the theater most of the seats were taken and we had to sit near the screen. The screen loomed above us like a cartoon tsunami. Then the lights in the theater dimmed, and our necks, cocked backward, bristled in anticipation of the images that would flood us with horror.

When the lights came back up I felt I had been bludgeoned. An innocent girl in a nightie had been a vessel for the most catastrophic force in the universe. Under Satan's dominion she had stabbed her vagina with a crucifix, vomited buckets of bile, rotated her head 360 degrees and spoke with a basso growl, lower even than Tennessee Ernie Ford's. (I heard later that those bellows were the slowed and amplified squeals of pigs being led to slaughter.) After all the self-mutilations, the gastric eruptions, the demonic ventriloquisms, a priest was summoned by the girl's frantic mother. Showdowns ensued between Good and Evil, and when the dust cleared, Good had won. I had forgotten, forget still, that Good had a presence, let alone a role in the outcome in the film. I could only replay the images of a girl undone by malevolence, as though those scenes had been puked onto my retinas, leaving me blind to little else.

That night I felt I had been sucked backward in time to those darker nights when, in a state of paralysis, I had play-acted at innocence. But where once Evil had been a threat from without—a werewolf or, say, a father—it now resided within, an invisible force ready, like fear itself, to leap out of my skin.

■ ■ ■

I can barely believe it was only a week ago when I received the call from Mrs. X, a distraught woman who asked to remain anonymous for reasons that I will soon make evident. So much has transpired since that time, so much indeed, that I scarcely feel myself to be the same man I was but only seven days ago. On that Monday my universe seemed as ordered to me as a furniture showroom. I am, or I should say was, a man of the cloth, a priest and professor of humanistic theology. Having a rather extensive background in both theology and psychology, I had felt myself to be an authority on the trappings of both the human mind and the human spirit. My life had been a monument to internal order. But nothing in all my many years of study, nothing in all my many indexes of scripture or symptomatology, could have prepared me for the storm about to rage through my life, strewing my life's work into chaos.

As I said, I received a message from Mrs. X last Monday on my answering machine. I had come home late after a dinner engagement with the dean of my department, Father Carson. I was pulling off my shoes, listening to the procession of usual greetings and reminders—my secretary, a few anxious students—when the most curiously guarded woman began pleading with me to meet her the following day. Her voice was as tight as the grip of someone at the edge of an abyss, and at certain pauses in her speech I could feel her thoughts plunge, like small rocks at her foothold, into an infinite dark. It is my duty, as a man of God, to answer the call of those in need, but I must confess, the undercurrent of fear and despair in her message was contagious, and I fell into bed only after double-locking all the locks in the house. Even so, my night was fitful. Shadows in the recesses of my bedroom congealed into a host of ugly faces, like the kind you see around the portals of medieval cathedrals, miserable stone ogres with pointed ears and pendulous tongues.

Finally, by about four, I was able to talk myself down. I knew these to be the vestiges of my childhood phobias, reason restored the shadows to themselves, and all the monsters that once roamed the orphanage of my boyhood receded into the past.

■ ■ ■

The Exorcist scared me more than any movie before or since. I spent the next three months trying to regain my composure, my moral foundation. I lived in a terror that my world might suddenly wrench itself from the fabric of predictability. Drips from a faucet might instantly fly upward, a closet door might unhinge and lunge toward me, slamming me against a wall, a car might drive itself. All these possibilities kept me in a state of perpetual anxiety, could verify that I too was possessed or at least insane—that I had, in either case, lost my self to chaos.

After all was said and done, after I recuperated, after I could trust my own mind, after I could put aside the shame of being undone by Hollywood, months after, one fact remained: in spite of whatever agnosticism I professed, deep down inside, I was still a little girl in a nightie, desperate to ward off Evil.

Generally the devil is portrayed as Pan, a taskmaster in red leotards, pitchfork at the ready, itching to goose the wicked back into the flames. Nothing too hair-raising, just an upright horned guy, warden of the underworld. He is, in effect, a crotchety Old Goat, not the proprietor of cosmic Evil, not that demon in *The Exorcist* who chewed up all the scenery and left the audience aghast.

Eager to flex their special effects, filmmakers often err in favor of revealing a demon's mug. When the forces of Christian magic get down to the real nitty-gritty, going to the mat with the forces of darkness, you'll be up to your ears in eye shadow and four-inch fingernails. It's my pentagram against your crucifix, chicken blood against holy water, prosthetic device versus prosthetic device. The demon's complexion might hit the spectrum anywhere from Spackle to hospital green, his pupils might be slit like a serpent's, he might have a stubby tail or a long oxen one with an arrowhead at the end, but he looks basically the same, as if Pan and Aget's famous gargoyle of Notre Dame had a baby. Bat ears, hound dog nose, a surplus of fangs. Requisite horns. Booga-booga. I'm seldom impressed.

At the instant when Evil drops its cloak, when the fake blood spatters and the makeup ends abruptly at the jawline, I exhale and sit back in my chair. Disbelief is no longer suspended.

I'm not suggesting that *The Exorcist* didn't have its fair share of special effects—I've seen it since and forced myself to catch all the gimmicks. Heaven knows that bedroom had hydraulic lifts and (nearly) invisible wires, and the girl's body, a dummy double, was rigged to contort into a chiropractor's nightmare. What cowed me about the Evil in *The Exorcist* was its immateriality, its ability to work like an invisible puppeteer, a maniacal Oz.

It's a big mistake to show the face of horror. Much better to keep the shark moving under the surface with only a peek of fin and that sawing bass viol—that'll squeeze your adrenals. The ghoulish excesses of special effects can't out-spook the almighty terror of the unforeseen, the unexamined, the unacknowledged.

■ ■ ■

The next morning I stood at the drive of Mrs. X's house, clean shaven, confident that whatever mishaps had befallen her, I would be able to salvage her faith in herself and in God. She had said little about her dilemma, only that her daughter had taken ill, but what illness it was, she had not disclosed. Cancer, I assumed. Something serious.

As I approached the front door I heard barking from an upstairs window. Mrs. X had obviously confined her dog in order that our conversation be undisturbed. For that I was eternally grateful. I had an uncanny dislike of dogs, with their disregard for order, their impossible slobbering, their ever-probing snouts. I rang the doorbell and smoothed my jacket. Almost instantly, Mrs. X opened the door and drew me into the foyer.

"Father, I am so relieved that you've come! Please excuse my appearance, I know I must look a sight! Let's go into the kitchen where we can talk . . . privately." She gave a little distracted look up the stairs toward what I believed to be the room where the dog was locked. His barking had become more vehement, more shall we say like a howl, and it was clear from the deepness of his voice that he was no small pooch. Probably one of those immense hounds bred for the hunting of bears.

At any rate, I followed Mrs. X down a long hallway into her kitchen. What little I could see of her house was dark, cold, like forgotten territory. Her kitchen, however, bore the evidence of her recent existence. Letters and teacups littered the counters. Sacks of groceries still lay on the table. Last night's supper, a hybrid of peas and something resembling oatmeal, lay uneaten, stacked on the top of a pile in the sink. Here was a woman who had time for little else but her sick child. Her life had shrunk to the size of her steaming teapot and whatever distance she covered on the dark path up the stairs to her daughter's bedroom.

She cleared a place at the table.

"Please, Father, sit down. There is so much to tell you, and I barely know where to begin. . . ." I sat down and looked up *into her face. In that instant she must have realized the shock I felt; she had the look of someone who had not slept in days, someone indeed, who might be found foraging in the streets, wild-eyed, afraid of the smallest noise. She drew her hand up to mask her frightfulness, and I looked away quickly, ashamed I had added to her grief. Then, with a gesture that seemed to lull our mutual embarrassment, she slowly folded a dishtowel and began her story.*

The first time I heard the voice of Evil I was four. Tennessee Ernie Ford, a country singer with a slack larnyx, sounded more like a tuba than a man as he moaned about how the company store owned the deed to his soul. When I asked my brother Stephen what the song meant he told me a story about a doctor named Faustus and a devil named Mephistopheles. I remember sitting in the front seat of my parents' two-tone '54 Chevrolet. I remember how the story frightened me, how the sun on the dashboard gave off a noxious smell, but I can't remember what Stephen said a soul was.

The notion that greed, ambition or even the itch to self-destruct could cause someone to lose a soul—an unknown but essential quantity—terrified me. I became suspicious of my own thoughts. My mind split in two. At one ear were the three angels of denial, those hear-no-evil-see-no-evil-speak-no-evil monkeys, desperate to perform their stunts and earn their candies. While at the other was the Beast, the eternal brat, trying to elbow its way to center stage. Particularly in situations that required me to play the part of sweetness and light, my own thoughts threatened to sell me into diabolical slavery, my very own thoughts became uncontrollable, softly chanting the word *penis* in a room full of cooing adults. It was Tourette's waiting to grab the mike.

At some point all children recognize their own potential for wickedness. They discover in the smorgasbord of language the power to cause great damage or simply to blaspheme. Bad words are to be hoarded in the arsenal of dirty diapers, in the toy box of bad spells. At night in the pastel bedrooms of the small and indignant, words like *penis* and *fuck-head* glow with preternatural incandescence.

The devil is the booking agent for that brat, setting up gigs, wheeling deals, making sure the contracts are signed and dated. The good mind tries to prevail as some kind of resident parent, King Solomon on the throne. Meanwhile there's an hysteric inside us, scraping together crucifixes and garlic necklaces, trying not to step on cracks in the sidewalk, ricocheting from desire to guilt to ritual behavior. But which character is the soul? Was the "me" in me the pontifical voice, or the voice that tried to coax me toward ruin?

■ ■ ■

"At first I thought it was some kind of allergic reaction . . ." Mrs. X shook her head.

"I took her to the best allergy specialists, put her on a very austere diet. But it didn't help. She only got worse, talking gibberish, screaming . . . the rest . . ."

"What 'rest'?" I pressed.

"You'll see soon enough, Father. Soon enough. Well, eventually I had to assume it might be psychological. I took her to some of the best neurologists, analysts, hypnotists, the gamut. Most wouldn't even work with her after the first visit. All of them thought it was my doing. 'Where did she learn that foul language?' or 'When did you start abusing your child?' I tell you, Father, I had nothing to do with it. Tiffany was always the sweetest, most well-behaved child, and now . . ."

The howling from the upstairs had grown most insistent, and at times fell over this woman's story like a suffocating and scratchy blanket. And it seemed that the harder I tried to listen to Mrs. X, the more horrid that yabbering became. And then finally it dawned on me! This vile racket I had attributed to some household pet was in fact the indecent bellowing of Mrs. X's sick child!

I took her hand in mine, but more to steady myself than to offer comfort, and I ironed my voice into an affect as smooth and as starched as my collar.

"Perhaps, madam, your little girl is suffering from . . . a rare disease called Tourette's syndrome. It is not difficult to control with the proper drugs and. . . ."

"Father, please, you must know why I've asked you here! I have nowhere else to turn. Believe me, I've tried every other possible explanation. There is no other way to rid her of it! And there's so little time. Please, help me Father. Get rid of it, before it destroys her!"

In her exasperation Mrs. X had thrown herself against my lap, her right hand clutching my thigh. I became instantly confused between the tremor that shot up my leg and the palpitations that were mounting inside me at the thought of her dreadful child. It was almost as if the fear of the moment had stirred the bulwark of my libido (or perhaps it was vice versa) and I broke into a sweat. In my haste to conceal the swelling in my trousers, I rose out of my chair and away from the danger spun by Mrs. X's hands. I mimicked the haste of one moved by the fires of battle, rather than one roused by the flames of lust. Squaring my jaw, bestowing a fatherly pat to Mrs. X's head, I marched back, through the dark tunnel that emptied itself at the foot of those ominous stairs.

The barking had stopped, and in its place a faint but wicked laugh, as though my flight from the heat of Mrs. X's fingers had been a cheap bit of bawdy comedy, a burlesque exit complete with oversize shoes. The demon was on to me. How could I mount my attack against it at such a disadvantage? I gripped the banister and began my ascent.

■ ■ ■

When I ask people what is Evil or does Evil exist most say it's a construct of human thought. Demons in your head and all that. Bad things happen in nature—typhoons, wildfires, ice ages—but they aren't evil. There's a difference between what allows us to commit acts of malevolence and what raises our hackles. The first, like cowardice, sports your best Sunday go-to-meetin' clothes, appears ever-agreeable, is everybody's bosom buddy; the latter, like death, wears the scariest of faces.

Betrayal, for example, is a hideous gorgon and is perceived as evil. We shrink from betrayal as though it were the cause of our suffering, rather than one of its effects. The social fabric unravels in an act of violence. A gentle father turns into a frothing drunk. A lover whose every gesture soothed you with familiarity suddenly has a whole new repertoire of manner-isms, foreign tastes, and talks on the phone sotto voce. Bottom line: suddenly the people you depend upon have distended canines, implants in the back of their heads and they speak in tongues.

Betrayal by the body feels evil. Disease is interpreted as a villainous conspiracy. We become superstitious at the sound of a sneeze. The word *cancer* is so darkly potent we dare not speak its name. Polio's plague in the fifties was a plague of hysteria. AIDS is now a scourge of entrenched ignorance. The demonizing of disease and of the diseased is as virulent today as it was in the Dark Ages. If you can't keep up, wuss, you're better off gone—or so goes the rationale of the lucky ones, the arrogance of those who've never been colonialized.

Invasion feels evil. Invaders, like the Vikings with their horned helmets, might have set the precedent for our Western devils. With the same approximation of dread, the same slow pacing of old horror films, post–World War II newsreels depicted the shadow of a Swastika eclipsing Europe's face.

Once an emblem of life's congruency, the Swastika became a badge of sinister intent; and Hitler, Evil incarnate. Hitler has reframed our discussions of Evil forever. So is Hitler the new reigning Old Goat, or rather, in the wisdom of vernacular, the current scapegoat? Take a second look at those so-called innocent folk during the war and you begin to recognize the ghoulish smiles of conspirators, the horns peeking out from the German citizenry, from the European closet collaborators, from Roosevelt, from the pope, from the whole cloven-footed lot.

What we dread we demonize, but this wasn't always so. People used to respect the agents of their terrors. To the horrific cave bear, early Europeans gave the mysteries of the seasons; to the lightning bolt, the highest eminence. To the marauding shark, Polynesians gave the enigma of fertility and renewal. Even the insane have their place in some societies, a bright thread in the woof and the weave.

■ ■ ■

When I opened the door at the top of the stairs I was struck dumb by the sight of a pretty girl propped up in her bed, peaceful as a lamb. Her lips were sweetly bowed, her long lashes batting like moths. A menagerie of stuffed animals lay scattered around her. One, a tiger, lay on its stomach, the key turning slowly in its back, Brahms's Lullaby tinkling into the blankets.

She was playing with me the way a cat toys with its victim before breaking its neck. And no sooner had I thought this than the toy tiger lifted its head and showed me its set of razor-sharp fangs.

All at once, as if opening a tin of rice and finding it suddenly squirming with larvae, the entire room seethed with demons. Every toy murmured and slurped, some gnashed their teeth at the sight of me, or snapped at the air, while others spun their limbs like propellers. Even the dresser showed its contempt for me by thrusting its drawers out, while the curtains splayed themselves shamelessly. And meanwhile, enthroned on her bed of soiled and shredded blankets, her pixilated toys writhing below her, the child let out a little bleat and her eyes rolled back into her head.

"Oh Father, please help me," she moaned, but not in the voice of a child . . . more, God help me, as her mother might. And I felt again the imploring hand of Mrs. X on my thigh as I stepped over the jumbles of copulating stuffed animals, and stood at the foot of that filthy bed.

"You Succubus!"

"Father, please, don't get so excited!" She was giggling and staring into my trousers. "Is that a psalm book in your pocket or are you just happy to see me?"

"Enough, Serpent!" I took a deep breath, ". . . though I walk through the valley of the shadow of death, I will fear no evil, for Thine is the . . ."

"Are you planning to live forever, Father? Ambition is attractive in a man." Her head arched back as she howled like a cartoon coyote, her lips as rounded as the bell of a bugle. Then her eyes latched onto mine and her breath closed around me like a malarial wind.

"Deathlessnesss is for the unborn. Blessed are those who are born in the sssnatch. All your sacrifice and Sunday ceremony can't save you from the throb of it. Flesshh is your ssscripture, heresssy your true face. . . ."

The diabolical sibilance was making my thoughts slippery, shaky . . . secular. Or was it shockular, sexual, slappery? I only knew I had to stop my head from spinning, ssssspinning . . .

I grasped the fiend by her shoulders and screamed, "Satan, take me!"

■ ■ ■

What is Evil? My childhood cruelties are more obvious. I taunted and slandered my little chums because—and this is no excuse—I hungered for power. As I grew older I became more sinister, my acts of evil more frequent, less easy to detect. I sold my soul for the glue of a common enemy or the drug of getting along. There are a hundred mean-spirited jokes I didn't confront. A thousand grudges I hoarded. A zillion or so communications I withheld. As for denial, who knows how many wounds I could have prevented, if only I had had the guts? In hindsight it wasn't necessary to always be right, yet at the time nothing could have been more coveted than that cloak and crown.

But confessions won't guarantee a restraining order. I've suspected for a while that Evil has taken up permanent residency in my household, has the run of the kitchen, the answering machine, the fax and the VCR. I don't like to acknowledge its presence. I'd rather pretend that everything's ducky when I turn out the lights. I shrink from looking over my shoulder, as though awareness itself was the blast before the mushroom cloud.

Catastrophe happens when we shun our dark gods, when they're sentenced to a life in the underworld. As we lie cringing in the dark, barely breathing, they loom ever larger in our closets. Eyes smoldering, their fangs grow longer, breath ranker.

■　■　■

The next thing I knew the child sat dumb-faced, blinking down at me. This was to be my great moment of piety, the kind priests pray for, an opportunity to lock horns with Beelzebub, the angel of the bottomless pit. I had laid down my life for the love of God. Now was I dead?

I was changed, but no angel's trumpet sounded, no feeling of Ascension lifted me skyward. No, in fact, I was incapable of raising myself from a heap on the floor. I seemed unable to use my legs, and I tugged at the useless things as if to wake them from dreaming. As I struggled to maneuver my bulk around the room, I was slapped with the truth—my knees were turned in the opposite direction, so that they bent backward! And as I flexed my shins—or were they now my hamstrings?—my lower legs sprung up in front of me like eager but unwanted children. But the most horrid aspect of my deformity was still taking shape in my brain, for at the tips of those limbs, beyond the droop of my pant legs, were hooves!

Dear Lord, what had happened to me? I absorbed something from the child, that much was clear. Was I like a hostage who soaks up the traits of a captor? Perhaps the child's dilemma had been only physiological, her neurons storming like firecrackers, and I with my haunted orphanage, magnified those sparks into my own Day of Judgment. Maybe I had taken on the madness that is childhood, and was still held by an hallucination of poly-morphous perversity. Or perhaps . . . I was . . . possessed.

It is not an easy task to learn to walk all over again, but I was motivated to leave this house as soon as I could. And so, clasping the bedpost, I pulled myself upright, swaying like a toddler. I found that by throwing the weight of my human half toward the dresser, my atavistic legs were obliged to follow suit, and I was able to wobble from one end of the room to the next. And in the course of twenty minutes, I was able to walk and trot, and scratch my underbelly with the use of my new-found legs.

Meanwhile I worried terribly for the child's mother who could only have grown more anxious at the stomping and scuf-fling on her kitchen ceiling. Dear God, what had I become?

Yet, my undertaking here had been a success, the child had fallen into an innocent sleep, a rest from the scourge of desires she was still too young to understand. She had been cleansed of her filth, no longer driven by impulses alone. She would be able now to keep her room in order, to eat politely, to maintain proper toilet habits, to behave in all ways with consideration and forethought. In short, I had resuscitated her future: dancing school, marriage, a family.

The tufts of hair on my rump itched terribly under my shorts, but I would simply have to ignore it until I got home. In the meantime there was Mrs. X, the vulnerable Mrs. X, whose breasts heaved in her moment of crisis. How would I navigate my way down the stairs and out her door without exposing the nature of my transformation? Indeed, what of Father Carson, my students, my secretary? My future in the clergy—rather, my new vocation as head satyr at the seminary—was ludicrous at best.

Nevertheless I decided to carry the child down to the fretting Mrs. X, with the conviction that my offering would redeem me in her eyes, however horrid I might appear. And in fact, my instincts proved correct. For no sooner did Mrs. X see her daughter bouncing in my arms, than she let out a great cry of relief, never noticing the monster who bore her child up, never once diverting her eyes from those rosy cheeks. And though my hooves clopped down the steps and my tail worked its way out of my pants, she never noticed that her priest had turned to were-goat. Mrs. X stood at the bottom of the staircase, her branching hands imploring me to deliver her daughter within the next heartbeat.

I bestowed the child upon her as though I had delivered her from the womb. No, I played it better than that. I was a bishop giving unction to the unclean, a pope laying a host on the tongue of a beggar. And though I found a familiar refuge in this masquerade, I could not stop my thoughts from stalking Mrs. X's hands, could not stop the hope that those hands would find their way back to my thigh. My tail began to sway salaciously, *and I recognized, for the first time, the utter sham of my devotions. Though I hated to tear myself from Mrs. X and her breasts, now heaving with maternal rapture, I made my exit.*

■ ■ ■

If I were to redesign the devil I'd strip him of his animal attributes and dude him up in the human spangles of hubris. I'd make him short, like Bonaparte or Ross Perot. His head and face would be abnormally small, allowing scant space for sensory organs. A grin would be the only prominent feature, a Pepsodent glare, branding one's eyes with its afterimage. He'd wink and say "darned" often, salute the flag like nobody's business. His voice would be irresistible, smooth as heroin, a voice-over voice that could roll in no time into evangelical thunder. He'd wear a monocle, a barrister's wig and an enormous codpiece. He would consist only of affect, like clothes with no emperor, a child feigning innocence.

On the other hand, if I could invent a conduit to a vital source, I'd draw a composite of creatures from which to take my inspiration: in my most wished for, most powerful form I would have the ears of a bat, the snout of a bloodhound, the palate of a grizzly bear. I'd have mongoose gumption, a beaver's pluck, the gape of a cat's pupils. Horns would be good, especially the endlessly spiraling ones of a wild old goat. Antennae, now that I think of it, might be nice too, and the ability to detect pheromones from a mile away. Give me the ear-to-ear grin of a porpoise, the precision of a bee, the active genitalia of a bonobo chimpanzee. Let me sing, a fathom lower than Tennessee Ernie Ford, like an elephant in the throes of estrus. Glue some dinosaur pituitary onto this collage, for sheer endurance on the planet; and for buttress and ballast, tail of kangaroo.

And for something humanoid in the mix, let me be on

intimate terms with my demons, with every nook and cranny of damnation. Give me a wicked laugh, and let me, God, pitch whatever's unexamined into the fiery, searing gaze of the mind.

■ ■ ■

I chose the least populated streets on my route home. I practiced my walk and pored over the events of that day. Had I become the new vessel of the Prince of Darkness? How, beyond this demi-goatness and the musk that stuck to me like a fog, was I changed? Oh, how could I say? I only knew that as I walked farther, and the breeze began to stir the leaves around me, I cared less and less.

I never noticed before the way leaves sound like whispering, beautiful whispering. And I could imagine children telling each other stories in the dark. Or lovers. In fact, every place visited in my imagination was as dark and as cozy as a pocket. And every bright corner that I turned on my walk seemed as welcoming as the nose of a mutt. Oh, I know it sounds too good to be true, like I've gone off the deep end, or it's the devil in me wanting to draw you in for the kill, but as I turned the corner of Fifth and Main, the throngs filling the city at rush hour, I had the most startling vision. I must have never seen people for who they are, must have only seen them as statistics, minds floating above the voids of their bodies. But now, now there were more hungers than I had names for, more appetites than I could ever hope to catalog.

And there was something else. Something wonderful. Among all the hips and calves and shirtsleeves, among the nylons, the wrists, and the lips, were . . . hooves. Hooves and tails, clambering above the pavement, flopping and bobbing in this sea of urbane fashion.

And how beautiful we looked, roaming free among the others, like thistles in a field of wheat, or pepper in a soup. We belonged to this world! And so, throwing off my collar, I stepped away from the shadows of that corner, eager to claim my place. I must have wandered for hours, down every major street in this city, shoulder to shoulder, my eyes flinting off the eyes of others, walking among the beasts and the gods.

WINGS

By November the Santa Anas are blasting. Mountains, once upstaged by smog, abruptly materialize. The air is Arctic bright, the sun a faceted topaz. Cars swerve to avoid wind-scattered palm fronds. If you can ignore your chapped skin, parched throat, the blood-marbled boogers that encrust tender nasal passages, you can appreciate this long-awaited change of season. This is the Angeleno's crocus, reprieve from an eon drenched in monochrome. We are a city suddenly reawakened.

My eyes open to the songs of birds. Birds that chatter at dawn's light, like an orchestra tuning up. Birds that trill from their pulpits in century plants. Jays and mockingbirds hoarsely contend their boundaries. Across the canyon a pair of red-tailed hawks screech while looping crazy eights around one another. Seagulls cyclone above the neighborhood market, blown in from the night's harangue. Were they swept inland from their nests on Anacapa Island? The city of birds careens above my own, its citizens running their errands, flirting, warring, hogging the limelight.

■ ■ ■

Only months ago the human city erupted into wide-scale rioting and Los Angeles burned for three days solid. On the second day of the civil unrest I took a walk to the top of my hill to view the destruction. Gunmetal plumes corkscrewed the air, big as tornadoes. There were more firestorms than I cared to count, Downtown, Industry, Baldwin Hills, West L.A., Koreatown. I wept to see parts of my city, my everyday landmarks, burn. When you live someplace it becomes a map of your soul, like those dreams of houses in which you discover new rooms. I was always in discovery of Los Angeles, and that discovery made me feel free, expansive within myself. But standing on that hill, the cityscape was redefined by chaos, boundaries were more tightly drawn, and I felt that my city, like my own life, was vulnerable to despair and extinction.

This is how the end of the world will look, I thought. Birds chirped at my back as if to say they would have no truck with it. You may fry, they sang, but life will go on. As it always has, they taunted, as it always has.

■ ■ ■

When the discovery of the fossil of *Archaeopteryx* was first publicized in 1861, it was met with anxious controversy. Only a few years had passed since Darwin published *The Origin of Species,* and the world was still smarting from the affront, reeling in denial, not yet ready to accept the secular powers of natural selection, much less trace a familiar avian form within the bones of a dinosaur's fossil. Only divine intervention could account for the gold gilt achievements of art, law or religion; only God could create this masterwork, prefab Adam, or that creature cloned from Adam's rib, Eve. The fossilized remains of marine life found in the mountains of Europe were simply proof that God had unleashed Noah's flood, nothing more.

But with *Archaeopteryx,* Bavarian limestone had preserved something altogether demonic. She looked like a mythological creature in miniature, had the head and legs of a small dragon, long tail feathers and wings of a phoenix. No bigger than a pigeon, she proved to be a missing link between Tyrannosaurus and the age of birds—a link between forests of ferns, ginkos and conifers, and the dazzling world of grasses, prairie flowers and honey bees.

Archaeopteryx moved through a flowerless world, a world without nectar or seeds or fruit, and she moved by running or, on occasion, by gliding. Her long feathers had not yet realized their genius in flight. Rather, they were used for insulation, to keep her blood warm. Our forebears, too, were warm-blooded, though far from being formed in a god's likeness, they were no bigger nor more beautiful than a rat.

■ ■ ■

Later this month I'll join my family for Thanksgiving dinner. At some point in that American meal someone digs the wishbone out of the desecrated bird, and challenges someone else to a duel of wishes. The wishbone, the clavicle, cemented the turkey's lineage with that of Tyrannosaurus; along with the feathers etched into that limestone slab, it was the confirmation that birds emerged from the dinosaur family.

If for nothing else, one should be thankful for our current position at the head of the food chain, thankful that we eat the turkey rather than are eaten by it, thankful that the age of dinosaurs is past. But let's not stop there. Before us are other epochs, each demanding countless changes of costume. With any luck we too might grow wings. Let's make a wish as we spar with fate, as we yank our half of the bone.

■ ■ ■

Occasionally a particular bird, usually a raucous jay, will make itself known to me, demanding a handout or warning me to stay clear of its nest. But largely birds form part of my ambiance, providing background color and music, like the neighbor's clock radio, or the maple tree, a liquid amber, now in a simmer across the street. Birdsongs accent my days and nights, yet those flavors are muted and muddied by my ignorance of them. Were I as tuned to those throats as I am to the voices in a piece of music, what a morning I'd hear!

Weeks ago I went to the library to learn more about birds, and I was surprised by how much material there was. As I read the titles, spine after spine, species announced themselves like cadets in a roll call: the Canada goose, the California quail, the wood duck, the ruffed grouse. The whooping crane, the hummingbird, the warbler. Jays, gulls, auks, hawks, crows, owls, eagles, egrets, petrels, puffins and budgies. The bushtit, the chickadee, the swan, and so on. More names than I had faces for.

At the library I discovered something curious, a paucity of information about the one bird continually under our very noses, in time, as it were, with our every step, who exists in every urban nook and cranny, except on the shelves of my library. Perhaps this is because the feral pigeon is not so much a creature of the air as a fixture of architecture, not so much the emblem of freedom as the symbol of urban decay. From shit brown to sharkskin, their plumage, like the garb of street crazies, runs the gamut from drab to garish. They have no song, just a moan, registering somewhere between desolate and wanton. I can't count the hours I've spent in hotel rooms, flat on my back, eyes on the ceiling, listening to the indecent coos of pigeons on the window ledges.

Like *Archaeopteryx* they represent something about ourselves we'd rather not acknowledge. Our fall from the realm of the angels. Dodging the wrath of traffic, pecking for encrusted scraps in the asphalt, they are like the legions of homeless people adrift on our boulevards. Their feast is our drek; our flotsam, their life raft.

Like the little fish feeding under the protective skirts of the

Man of War, pigeons have a symbiotic relationship to our cities. With their talons as grimy as tire treads, their pupils as dark as the slag buckets of bygone industries, they are an urban nightmare scuttling out into the light of day. The city's filth is mirrored back to us. It is estimated that two-thirds of the pigeons in Paris are infected with psittacosis, or parrot fever, that each resident of New York City inhales three micrograms of dried pigeon fecal dust a day.

Like rats, they have become specialized to survive the urban environment. Though they have few taste buds they have shown an ability to detect chemical substances in water at low concentrations. They see symbols, take visual clues. Animal behaviorists have run tests in which pigeons were able to recognize two-dimensional stylized symbols, to equate, for example, the international symbol for man with a human being. They have learned to avoid red-colored objects. They live in small communities, one guards while the others sleep. They are streetwise. To my mind they show an uncanny ability to dodge cars, to waddle unhurried until, at the last possible moment, they lift themselves from an oncoming tire. Occasionally I see an exception to that rule. Just last week, I found a dead pigeon at the 7-Eleven, a casualty of the parking lot, flat as a ceremonial Apache headdress, its cache of seeds scattered over its splayed carcass.

■ ■ ■

Rock pigeons, ancestors of the feral pigeon, once toddled and flapped through the streets of Alexandria, Thebes, Constantinople. Dating back to the dovecotes in ancient Egypt, where they were raised for food, rock doves are the oldest domesticated animals.

Pigeons come from a large family of birds, the *Columbidae*. The pigeon's most revered sibling is the homing pigeon, a friend to spies, a wonderment to the scientists of navigation. The world's champion homing pigeon, Sandringham Lightning, is owned by the world's richest woman, the queen of England. Then there's the doe-eyed sister, the mourning dove, cooing like a Halloween ghost along the drives of suburbia. Or that family member with the spiritual calling, the albino dove bearing the olive branch, out from under the storm, across the floodwater, signaling the end of cataclysm.

Whenever my father returned from his hunting trips in Willows, California, bloody sack in hand, my mother would pull out the corn meal and the cast iron skillet, and by dinner time she'd emerge from the kitchen with a platter of dove stew. The tiny prone bodies lay on a mattress of polenta, blanketed in a rich brown gravy. And as I savored the malty flavor of their bite-size breasts, my teeth would inevitably clamp on a bead of dad's buckshot.

Consider squab, a moniker for pigeon, elevated nevertheless to an aristocratic entree. It may be hard to imagine eating a pigeon, one of those "flying rats." But how far could it be, plucked and browned, toxins and parasites excluded, from an identical carcass of squab? Wouldn't it taste the same, gamy and deep, drenched in a garlicky roux?

Barely over a century ago another cousin, the passenger pigeon, soared in gargantuan flocks over North America. My great-grandfather, a lumberman in Michigan, must have witnessed those endless clouds as they applauded overhead, eclipsing the sun, two billion strong. But soon lumbermen and developers and hunters cut these hordes to a paltry few until, on the eve of the First World War, the last passenger pigeon, Martha, died in the Cincinnati Zoo.

There seems to be no end in sight for our squalid flying rat, sparing global disaster. As long as there are buildings, especially stone ones, or ones with ledges, or awnings, archways or porticos; as long as there are statues, gargoyles or fountains; as long as there are overpasses, stoplights, town squares; as long as there are rooftops and sidewalks, there will be those invincible birds.

If evolution can switch the thunder step of Stegosaurus into the flutter of a whippoorwill, if leathery scales reconfigure into down, if adaptation can make it possible for pigeons to thrive in our deadly cities, what might be *our* transformation? However this world may end, will some shrunken cousin of ours survive, a small creature flying through the porticos of the future, scrambling for the crumbs of the reigning giants?

■ ■ ■

In dreams I fly, not with the use of wings, but rather as though I were swimming, my arms stroking currents of air until I rise over my mother's house, my old schoolyard, telephone poles, outlying farms, and finally trees. I fly as if I were the cloned offspring of Mary Martin and Diana Niad. Swimming is the more familiar form of suspension, a locomotion that nearly defies gravity. Perhaps the memory survives even from our time in the womb, or earlier still in the primal sea. Though we're now creatures of land, we can't shake the kinesthesis, the sensation of buoyancy; it's like a phantom limb. We imagine we can glide through the stratosphere. All cultures have depicted people with wings. Our species yearns to colonize the air, as though that element alone could house our spirits.

Angels descend from the heavens bringing inspiration, commandments, apocryphal messages. In the Annunciation, one of the most painted images involving angels, the archangel Gabriel appears to the Virgin, holding a white Easter lily, bearing the seed of the holy ghost. This is the moment of conception, divine conception in its myriad meanings.

For my money, the best Annunciation is Leonardo da Vinci's. It doesn't pander to the idea of modesty, or any twisted Western notion of sexual restraint. The Virgin is not covering her cleavage or having a vapor or averting her eyes. Da Vinci's Mary is head-on with the angel. Like a Buddha in the mirror, her palm faces the angel's in the same holy Ping-Pong of a greeting. The eyes are as fixed on each other as Ikhnaton's is on the infinite, a reckoning. These two are, after all, preparing themselves for creation.

What must it feel like, I wonder, to anticipate such an angel? Like my unblinking stare toward the illuminated screen of my computer? toward these words, toward some tumult of wings?

■ ■ ■

There are, or so the story goes, fallen angels. Those who were expelled from the stratosphere, as we were from the Garden. It is said that these vain ones fell through hubris into the fiery pit. And all the outlaw pagan deities fell with them, under the ground, under the rug. More shadows lurking beneath the surface than even Jung could shake a stick at.

With their insignia bat wings, perky genitals and angry eyes, demons bring on adultery, greed, the unraveling of the social fabric. Yet let's face it, devils can also work wonders. Their gifts of torment temper the mind; thoughts become sharper, resolve, stronger. We may have been sullied, bruised even, but when the battles are over, we are, like Nietzsche, made stronger.

Of course, no one would want to be trapped for all eternity with the damned. Think of it, the endless grind, erosion of all hope, never a fresh breath of air in those incessant flames.

■ ■ ■

Even before the civil disturbance of '92, fire was this city's element. Every fall arsonists set the hills ablaze, ash drifts down in the mornings like a mist, powdering windshields, dusting the surface of my bird bath. But with the riots, ash and the sour smell of smoke came early. In all, a thousand fires raged over a three-day period, and god knows what chemicals were set loose into the atmosphere.

The *Los Angeles Times* ran many first-person accounts of the riots, otherwise known as the L.A. uprising, the L.A. revolt and the L.A. disaster. Like the blind men feeling the elephant, each person perceived her/his own animal. Each interview was a testament of how persons felt backed into their own corners of desperation. Many would, if they didn't already, arm themselves. The ante was upped.

By the second night, my eyes bleary from thirty hours of television news watching, I caught a bird's-eye view of Western Avenue. Fires opened up like poppies, and nodded their fevered heads north, an illuminated arrow pointing to my home in the hills, a red carpet unraveling toward my doorstep. My windows and doors were shut tight of course, and double-checked, but there was no keeping out the smoke. No denying my city was mad as hell. With the riots, the era of denial in Los Angeles had, in fact, reached obsolescence. And I realized that if I'm not careful, my white person's larder of paranoia, guilt and denial would conspire to make me as fossilized as a dinosaur. The beacons raging along the avenues were every Angeleno's summons: if we don't reawaken to one another, the whole city could go down under striations of cinder and rubble.

Curfew had been in effect for hours. Except in the hot spots, the city of angels had never seemed so deserted. But soon creatures, skunks and possums, waddled down the middle of my street, unmindful of the tensions that had created the calm.

By morning, the sky eerily yellow from ash, birds started up their songs, like clockwork. They foraged for their nesting materials, performed their acrobatics, vanished behind a veil of green. I ventured out onto Hollywood Boulevard, where pho-tographers were competing for the best shots of char. Shopkeepers and their neighbors had already swept the streets of debris and broken glass. And pigeons had begun picking tid-bits from the cooling wreckage.

Of all the city's creatures, I thought, the pigeons are its phoenix. There are the other birds, prettier, more clever per-haps, with real songs to sing. But it's the feral pigeons who embody sheer perseverance, pecking through the rubble of burned-out minimalls, rising from the city's ash, from the swel-ter of the blacktop. That indomitable bird will thrive however long we stave off Armageddon. From oily gutters, diesel on their wings, lifting into a volatile sky.

ABOUT BEING AWAKE WHILE DRIVING FROM MY HIGH SCHOOL REUNION

Interstate 5 slices California's Central Valley headlong. The main corridor between San Francisco and L.A., I-5 persists surveyor-straight. On a June scorcher, without a good conversationalist to ride shotgun, I am returning home from my twenty-fifth high school reunion. Though my spine is lodged in one position, and the road is aimed like a blade at the horizon, my thoughts meander like rivulets in a landscape. They lap at the reunion, they swirl around the faces of old friends, around the numbers on the odometer, but mostly they surge around time itself.

I am driving through a landscape made up of six hours, the way a lovesick astronaut would travel light-years to get back to her beloved. I can't help but parcel up this tortoise of a drive, open a new stick of gum at every third rest stop, eat a cookie every hundred miles, fracture the monotony by playing little games with the clock. As I approach three hours, when the trip becomes airless and claustrophobic, I'm aware of the ways in which my time is piddled away. This, I pray, isn't a metaphor for how my life is lived.

I began in Northern California. I lived the first half of my life there; the latter, adult half in Southern California.

Before moving to Los Angeles twenty-four years ago, I was warned how Angelenos were a vain and tacky lot, and while much of that warning proved true, those qualities are as much the population's glory as its downfall. Tackiness can be a pleasant respite from the parochial airs of San Francisco, and southern narcissism seems sunny compared to the north's Victorian restraint. Northern Californians consider their part of the state ordered, sophisticated, verdant; while for them, the southern part is sheer vulgarity, parched both culturally and geographically.

When I moved to the barbarous Southland I traded a city for a suburban megalopolis, redwoods for Joshua trees, my moorings for a coming of age. Most of my family is still up in the Bay Area as well as old friends from my high school days, their complexions preserved by coastal fog. I fantasize about moving back up, back to a world of moist skin, clean air and, for better or for worse, the past.

When I left Northern California I was at the peak of my physical development, no cell was more perfectly made, no nerve more finely tuned. My thymus gland, the seat of my immunity, was still robust and—scary to contemplate—I was never better suited to conceive new life. Yet, in spite of my physical vigor, I lived half-asleep. The past was a burden I shouldered with an indolent slouch. My father's legacy—to live out one's days in a never-neverland of novels and bourbon—would likely dictate my future, case closed. There were other causes for resignation: I had seen my father's tantrums detonate our kitchen like a test site in Nevada, and learned to not speak of it. Bowing and scraping to my own personal patriarch, I was held hostage by the hush of my own home. I knew well how to duck and cover, how to keep a secret. So it was convenient that when I suspected I was queer—a booger on the family tea set—I was already on my way to becoming invisible. Wouldn't parents snatch their children to their sides when they saw me coming their way? Wouldn't the tabloids show my picture at the check-out counter? I must not stand out, I was made for lesser things.

When I first drove south twenty-four years ago I was lethargic, still adolescent, certain my virginity would persist throughout my lonely life, certain that the value of learning anything new was nil. My young past may have been only pint-size, but it severely curtailed my mobility, my sense of possibility, like a carry-on bag filled with lead.

■ ■ ■

Making the drive in the winter months, when the Valley's moisture clots into a tulle fog, your headlights bore barely a car's length into the custard. Much of the Central Valley used to be wetlands, but in the last thirty years, as a result of over-farming, the San Joaquin is dusty. When the fall wind kicks up, dust can be just as opaque as fog. Car accidents on the interstate quickly accrete—ten, twenty crashes in a bunch—and are often fatal.

Before reaching Coalinga, the midway point, you pass the Harris Ranch. Even in one of those impenetrable Valley fogs, when the windows offer nothing but a blank page, there's no mistaking the reek of cow shit. You know thousands of cattle are out there, waiting to die. I call the Harris Ranch the Cow Dachau, not to minimize the horror of the camps, but to heighten the nightmare that is this slaughterhouse. It is impossible to drive by that wasteland and not imagine oneself as a steer, standing in one's own crap, knees locked, resigned to both the monotony and to the slaughter that will end the monotony.

I think back a quarter of a century to my father slumped in his reading chair. To me, home from school and itching to run to the rumpus room to hear the new Beatles' LP, the book on the lap of that man in the living room was the black hole of my universe. Books were traps into which a person could become engulfed, the props of monotony, time wasted. Like his booze, books were a compulsion, withdrawal from the life orbiting around him. Of course, what was the Beatles' "Don't Bother Me," or "I'm a Loser" but a relief from the agonies of my own adolescence?

As a teenager I saw an artist's rendering of the Beatles, then in their early twenties, as they would look in their fifties. The drawings of the four prunish codgers in their moth-eaten collarless jackets were preposterous, obscene. The Beatles, like me, would never grow old, at least not like *that*. I couldn't imagine my face in fast-forward, like the time-lapse films of exploding blossoms, my face a bloom of radiating creases, an avalanche of jowls.

Now in the mirror I watch as my throat rumples like last night's pillowcase. I see the frown lines slump from the corners of my mouth and recall my father's scowl over the top of his book. Like him, I have been swallowed into the universe of words, while time reels around me.

Is it possible to live completely in the present? To be awake to each second as though it were the last?

■ ■ ■

Once I was a manuscript of short unedited sentences, a new tablecloth, a fresh roll of film. I relished my own physical perfection. But time would abrade me. Sun would drizzle me with pigment until my back was a canvas by Jackson Pollock. Habits would codify me, and circumstance carve deep cuts of character.

As a child I'd perform for you the Shirley Temple pout, the gap-tooth grin, the see-no-evil. Innocence was a mere minstrel show. I played nostalgia to my audience of elders, became a conduit through which they revisited the haunts of time-gone-by. This was my power, manipulative, pitifully brief.

To see me then—coltish, dolphin bellied, nipples like pudding skin—you might have detected a critic smug with inexperience. Part of me stood in contempt of the aging around me. Part of me took offense at the scars aggregating on the knees of my older siblings. Part found the calluses growing on my mother's feet as alien as the hooves on a pachyderm. I scorned those white-haired ogres who inched down a staircase I ascended, two, three steps in a bound. Experience was the enemy, would bring on the siege of erosion, of gravity, of inevitable scarcity. I was loathe to dip even one piggie into the current of time, for fear of diluting my diminishing magic, or of being swept away.

Now, having dunked, having been swept up, I'm merely trying to, as the saying goes, tread water. My hair has gone white. Daylight appears, then just as swiftly, fades. I wolf my morning cereal, sit down to write, barely finish a paragraph before it's time to make dinner. And all the while the second hand whirs like the blade of a propeller.

Once upon a time each moment glowed like a brand-new cell; experience was acquisitive, and memory flexed its nimble fingers. I was either stalled in the languor of new sensations, or aching for the second hand to tug itself free from one numeral and lodge itself onto the next.

■ ■ ■

Be Here Now was the slogan of the sixties. It was, to some extent, my generation's last bleat before getting the boot from childhood's garden. As a teenager in that era, I once smoked some tainted marijuana and found myself trapped in the NOW. When the dope hit I had just dropped the needle on Janis Joplin. "Take it," she implored, as though she were offering me one more slice of pie. "Take another little piece of my heart, now baby." Her third heaarrtt scratched the ceiling and refused to collide with the next syllable. I fell back onto the bed, aware that the lapse between intervals was widening into a gap as far as the space between myself and the kitchen. The glue of temporality was coming undone. NOW was impulse without linkage, a desert of exclamation points, a relentless procession of unrelated sounds. NOW offered no melody, no dynamics, no rhythm. Chronology, I realized, was like gravity, it held the fragments of the world together. I wanted to have the world back. I waited to escape that pandemonium, to be rescued by a future, which was, I prayed, an end to meaningless noise. Somewhere in that room, I knew, Janis Joplin was still pleading for recognition. I waited like the cows of Coalinga, like those who endure unbearable, discordant stretches of time. I floated like an astronaut hoping to be let back into the capsule, to be held once more within the insulation of continuity, to be assured of the world. When at last I came down from the effects of that chemistry, when I was straight, so to speak, I was resolved to live in something other than NOW.

There is a kind of present known to athletes as *the zone*. To be in the zone—a past-present-future all-of-a-piece kind of time—is to be fully awake, performing at your peak, absorbing the details of each hurdle before you clear the bar. Performers sometimes call this state *being in your body*. Straying from an awareness of your body onstage might allow your delivery to go flat; while being zeroed into, say, your heartbeat is to rediscover each phrase with renewed emotion, to anticipate the audience's next breath. We're all familiar with how doubt, resignation and habit conspire in making our accomplishments merely adequate, at best; but are we acquainted with how to reenter our bodies, inhabit the present like nobody's business, swing like the instruments in a quartet, in tune, in a groove, all the parts working together? It's no easy feat to keep one's mind riveted in the present, to have at all times your eye on the ball and your feet at the plate. The mind is lazy and wanders; the mind is vain and obsesses.

It is often said that we use only a small percentage of our brains. What on earth are we doing that we keep the rest of the house dark and empty? Our synapses firing the same old same old? Reciting the tired saws that time equals money, a rolling stone gathers no moss, it's a dog-eat-dog world? Let's assume for the moment that the remainder of the brain is reserved for *the zone*. For a good game of tennis played to the fullest. A six-hour car ride in which the same old same old is made new. In that kind of present we are giving of ourselves, running another lap, going for the orgasm, singing our words. And here's that great collision of meanings in the word *present*, a verb, and two nouns.

■ ■ ■

Everything contains a partial record of its past within itself—the rocks of the Coastal Mountains carry a record of their days in the sea, my great-grandmother's inner ear resonates in the spirals of my DNA, the egg carries the makings of a chicken.

The future remains, nevertheless, perpetually invisible. It is expressed in the present tense, nascent, vibrant, but as yet immaterial. Perhaps if we were a little less devoted to the past, a little less sure of what we know, we'd be able to catch our future's spectral outline emerging, and we'd follow that phantom into an explosion of possibility.

Since the Gregorian Calendar we've envisioned the temporal realm as a straight arrow trajectory, one day clacking against the next like an endless trail of dominoes. Christ's birth and death forever straightened the seasonal spiral into the march of time. But suppose the plots of our lives were more interconnected, more three-dimensional, a mosaic of interlocking gears. Suppose we were to travel backward to the initial moment, the mother gear—the Big Bang—what would be there but the possibility of everything? Suppose the future existed before time began? Suppose if we could journey backward—drawkcab—to that initial moment in time, the time at which scientists are synchronizing their clocks, Planck time—10^{-43} second—the germination of existence, what else could there be but the future, huge, looming with potential?

Returning on I-5 from the reunion, I am gaining on an onion truck, the skins shucked off by the wind, chafing my windshield, sputtering off into the air like white butterflies. The radio blathers about redemption, how the door to heaven is narrow, Visa and MasterCards accepted. Dust devils scour the valley floor.

All of us these days are on the road to somewhere, neither where we came from nor quite where we're going, barely able to stay awake. It seems I've spent my life hoping to free experience from the past, to peel away layers of habit, applied meaning, and let living breathe, to allow the future to hit me like a blast of fresh air. I pass another onion truck, and though I smell the sweet reek of the onions, I am concentrating on seeing the truck as the source of the world's white butterflies.

Fifty miles inland, on a course than runs parallel to the San Andreas Fault, I'm reminded of the pace of geological time. My life, seen from such a tempo, would exist in the blinking of an eye, in less than a nanosecond, less than a frame in which the film of plate tectonics is played. In this film, pieces of land drift from the Pacific toward the western edge of North America where they collide, like the traffic pileups at Coalinga, creating the mosaic of California, pushing up rocks to form the Central Valley and the Coastal Mountain Range.

Likewise, the Milky Way and its nearby galaxies are drifting toward a common destination, clustering, speeding toward something called the Great Attractor. We, like the Whos in Horton's world, are crammed onto a mote in that gargantuan voyage. We are making a ruckus, carrying on, barely able to hear one another, unaware of our passage through the Abyss.

At the reunion I had gone for a walk. I climbed the hill behind the gym, the hill everyone used to visit for a smoke or a good cry. There had been a view of the school from the top where an oak tree offered shade from the afternoon's glare. When I reached the oak I ran my hand along the corrugations of the bark, picking out the butts of recently smoked cigarettes, and trying to catch my breath. Below me was the picture I remembered—the roofs of classrooms and dorms connected by a ribbon of pathways—the aerial view of the small life I once lived. At that time the sight of a friend or of a special teacher ambling below me had made my heart leap into my throat. Now strangers meandered along the paths and meant nothing. My eyes moved upward toward the horizon, away from the foothills of Mount Diablo, toward the north, the west and the south. The Coastal Range spread out before me in undulations of golds of greens, a dazzling view I had never seen until that moment. "Jesus," I panted, "how on earth did I miss all this?"

That night at dinner my old friends had asked me, Was I happy? Would I have children? What is my book about? Some asked, with typical Northern California arrogance, why I live where I do. We all made jokes about aging, though most of us agreed that age had made us less unconscious, more awake. After dinner we raised our glasses in memory of those who had died, and each of us faltered just a second before the clink.